First World War
and Army of Occupation
War Diary
France, Belgium and Germany

30 DIVISION
90 Infantry Brigade
Manchester Regiment
16th Battalion
7 November 1915 - 17 June 1918

WO95/2339/1

The Naval & Military Press Ltd
www.nmarchive.com
Published in association with The National Archives

Published by

The Naval & Military Press Ltd

Unit 10 Ridgewood Industrial Park,

Uckfield, East Sussex,

TN22 5QE England

Tel: +44 (0) 1825 749494

www.naval-military-press.com

www.nmarchive.com

This diary has been reprinted in facsimile from the original. Any imperfections are inevitably reproduced and the quality may fall short of modern type and cartographic standards.

© **Crown Copyright**
Images reproduced by permission of The National Archives, London, England, 2015.

Contents

Document type	Place/Title	Date From	Date To
Heading	WO95/2339-1		
Heading	30th Division 90th Infy Bde 16th Bn Manchester Regt Nov 1915-Jun 1918 To 14 Div 42 Bde.		
Miscellaneous	From Officer Commanding, 16th (S) Bn. Manchester Regiment.	30/11/1915	30/11/1915
Heading	30th Division Nov 15 June 18 16th Manchester Vol I 121/7635.		
War Diary	Larkhill.	08/11/1915	08/11/1915
War Diary	Larkhill.	07/11/1915	07/11/1915
War Diary	Boulogne	08/11/1915	09/11/1915
War Diary	St. Riquier.	10/11/1915	16/11/1915
War Diary	Brucamps.	17/11/1915	17/11/1915
War Diary	Villers Bocage.	18/11/1915	27/11/1915
War Diary	Bowneville.	28/11/1915	30/11/1915
Operation(al) Order(s)	16th M/R Operation Order No. 1.	27/11/1915	27/11/1915
War Diary	Bonneville.	01/12/1915	08/12/1915
War Diary	Hebuterne.	08/12/1915	14/12/1915
War Diary	Bonneville.	15/12/1915	31/12/1915
Operation(al) Order(s)	16th Manchester Regiment-Operation Order No. 2. by Lieut. Col. Petric. D.S.O.		
Operation(al) Order(s)	16th Manchester Regiment-Operation Order No. 3. by Lieut Col. Petric. D.S.O.	06/12/1915	06/12/1915
Operation(al) Order(s)	Operation Orders No. 4 By Lieut-Col. C.L.R. Petrie, D.S.O. Commanding 16th (S) Bn. Manchester Regiment.	13/12/1915	13/12/1915
Miscellaneous	Attachment Of 16th Batt. The Manchester Regiment.	04/12/1915	04/12/1915
Heading	3rd Div 16th Manchester Vol 3		
War Diary	Bonneville.	01/01/1916	04/01/1916
War Diary	Maricourt.	05/01/1916	20/01/1916
War Diary	Suzanne.	21/01/1916	27/01/1916
War Diary	Maricourt.	28/01/1916	30/01/1916
War Diary	Maricourt A 3 Sector.	30/01/1916	31/01/1916
Heading	16th S. Bn Manchester Regt (1st City) War Diary Vol I. February 1916. 16th Manchester Vol:4.		
War Diary	Suzanne.	01/02/1916	05/02/1916
War Diary	Maricourt.	06/02/1916	06/02/1916
War Diary	A 3 Sub-Sector.	07/02/1916	07/02/1916
War Diary	Maricourt A 3 Sub-Sector.	08/02/1916	11/02/1916
War Diary	Suzanne.	12/02/1916	16/02/1916
War Diary	New A I Sub Sector.	17/02/1916	20/02/1916
War Diary	Suzanne.	21/02/1916	23/02/1916
War Diary	F 3 Sub Sector.	24/02/1916	25/02/1916
War Diary	Suzanne.	26/02/1916	27/02/1916
War Diary	Y 3 Sub Sector.	28/02/1916	29/02/1916
Heading	16 Manchester Vol 5 XXX (90)		
War Diary	Y 3 Sub-Sector.	01/03/1916	01/03/1916
War Diary	Suzanne.	02/03/1916	04/03/1916
War Diary	Y 3 Sub-Sector.	05/03/1916	07/03/1916
War Diary	Suzanne.	08/03/1916	11/03/1916
War Diary	Y 3 Sub-Sector.	12/03/1916	15/03/1916

War Diary	Suzanne.	16/03/1916	17/03/1916
War Diary	Bray.	18/03/1916	28/03/1916
War Diary	Corbie.	29/03/1916	13/04/1916
War Diary	Coisy.	14/04/1916	14/04/1916
War Diary	Breilly.	15/04/1916	29/04/1916
War Diary	Corbie.	30/04/1916	30/04/1916
War Diary	Camp Bois.	01/05/1916	01/05/1916
War Diary	Celestins Suzanne.	01/05/1916	02/05/1916
War Diary	Y 33 Sub-Sector.	03/05/1916	08/05/1916
War Diary	Suzanne.	09/05/1916	14/05/1916
War Diary	Y 3 Sub-Sector.	15/05/1916	19/05/1916
War Diary	Suzanne.	20/05/1916	25/05/1916
War Diary	Y 3 Sub-Sector.	26/05/1916	01/06/1916
War Diary	Camp Etinehem.	02/06/1916	10/06/1916
War Diary	Z 1 Sub Sector.	11/06/1916	17/06/1916
War Diary	Le Mesge.	18/06/1916	21/06/1916
War Diary	Oissy.	22/06/1916	26/06/1916
War Diary	Etinehem.	27/06/1916	30/06/1916
Heading	July 1916.		
Miscellaneous	A the national archives.		
Heading	War Diary of 16th Bn. Manchester Regt. for July 1916.		
War Diary	Mantauban	01/07/1916	01/07/1916
War Diary	Happy Valley.	02/07/1916	09/07/1916
War Diary	Montauban Area.	09/07/1916	11/07/1916
War Diary	Maricourt.	11/07/1916	11/07/1916
War Diary	Bois Celestins	12/07/1916	13/07/1916
War Diary	Dadurs.	14/07/1916	23/07/1916
War Diary	Cambridge Copse.	24/07/1916	29/07/1916
War Diary	Trones Wood.	31/07/1916	31/07/1916
War Diary	Mansel Copse.	31/07/1916	31/07/1916
Miscellaneous	16th (S) Battalion, Manchester Regiment. Report on Guillemont Operations July 29/31 1916	29/07/1916	29/07/1916
Miscellaneous	Brief Report of Operations carried out by 16th Manchester Regiment On July 1st/2nd. Appendix I.	03/07/1916	03/07/1916
Heading	90th Brigade. 30th Division. 1/16th Battalion Manchester Regiment August 1916.		
War Diary	Mansel Copse.	01/08/1916	31/08/1916
War Diary		28/08/1916	31/08/1916
Heading	War Diary. For The Month Of September. 16th Bn. Manchester Regiment. Lieut-Col. Commanding 16th (S) Bn. Manchester Regiment. Volume XI.		
War Diary	Essars.	01/09/1916	02/09/1916
War Diary	Festubert.	03/09/1916	14/09/1916
War Diary	Bethune.	16/09/1916	16/09/1916
War Diary	Busnette.	17/09/1916	17/09/1916
War Diary	Beauval.	18/09/1916	20/09/1916
War Diary	Flesselles.	21/09/1916	30/09/1916
Operation(al) Order(s)	16th (S) Bn. Manchester Regiment Operation Orders Number G. 4. By Lieut. Col. H. Knox Commanding 16th (S) Battalion Manchester Regiment. Appendix I.	02/09/1916	02/09/1916
Operation(al) Order(s)	Operation Order No. G.5 by Lt. Col. H. Knox. Commanding 16th Manchester Regt. Appendix II.	07/09/1916	07/09/1916
Operation(al) Order(s)	Operation Orders No. G. 7. By Lieut. Col. H. Knox. Commanding Elsie. Appendix III.	14/09/1916	14/09/1916

Heading	War Diary For The Month Of October. 16th Bn. Manchester Regiment. 3-10-1916. Major Commanding 16th (S) Bn. Manchester Regiment. Volumn XII.		
War Diary	Flesselles.	01/10/1916	04/10/1916
War Diary	Buire.	05/10/1916	10/10/1916
War Diary	Trenches.	11/10/1916	19/10/1916
War Diary	Montauban Camp.	20/10/1916	22/10/1916
War Diary	Ribemont.	23/10/1916	26/10/1916
War Diary	Sus-St-Leger.	27/10/1916	31/10/1916
Miscellaneous	16th (S) Battalion Manchester Regiment. Casualties October 1916 Appendix I.	02/11/1916	02/11/1916
Heading	War Diary For The Month Of November. 16th Bn. Manchester Regiment. 5-12-1916. Captain, Commanding 16th (S) Bn Manchester Regiment. Volume XIII.		
War Diary	Trenches.	01/11/1916	05/11/1916
War Diary	Bailleulval.	06/11/1916	11/11/1916
War Diary	Trenches.	12/11/1916	17/11/1916
War Diary	Bellacourt.	18/11/1916	23/11/1916
War Diary	Trenches.	24/11/1916	30/11/1916
Heading	War Diary. For The Month Of December 16th Bn. Manchester Regiment. 2-1-1917. Lieut. Colonel, Commanding 16th (S) Bn. Manchester Regiment. Volume XIV.		
War Diary	Bailleulval.	01/12/1916	31/12/1916
Operation(al) Order(s)	Operation Order No G.14 By Captain R.E. Roberts Commanding 16th (S) Battalion Manchester Regiment.		
Miscellaneous	O.C. 18th Manchester.		
Operation(al) Order(s)	Operation Order No. G. 13 By Captain R.E. Roberts, Commanding 16th (S) Battalion, Manchester Regiment.	05/12/1916	05/12/1916
Operation(al) Order(s)	Operation Order No. G. 16 By Capt. R.E. Roberts, Commanding 16th (S) Battalion, Manchester Regiment.	23/12/1916	23/12/1916
Miscellaneous	O.C. 18th Manchester.		
Heading	War Diary. For The Month Of January. 16th (S) Battalion, Manchester Regt. 1-2-17. Lt. Col., Commanding 16th (S) Bn. Manchester Regiment Volume XV.		
War Diary	Halloy.	01/03/1917	12/03/1917
War Diary	Grenas.	12/03/1917	18/03/1917
War Diary	Monchiet.	19/03/1917	19/03/1917
War Diary	Trenches.	21/03/1917	28/03/1917
War Diary	Bellacourt Grosville.	29/03/1917	31/03/1917
Heading	War Diary. For The Month Of February. 16th (S) Battalion, Manchester Regiment. March 2nd 1917 Lieut-Colonel Commanding 16th (S) Bn. Manchester Regiment. Volume XVI.		
War Diary	Daineville.	01/02/1917	28/02/1917
Heading	War Diary 16th (S) Bn Manchester Regiment. Volume XVII March-1917. Lieut-Colonel Commanding 16th (S) Bn Manchester Regiment. Vol 17		
War Diary	Trenches.	01/01/1917	31/01/1917
Heading	War Diary For The Month Of April 16th (S) Battalion Manchester Regiment Volume XVIII.		
War Diary	Grosville.	01/04/1917	01/04/1917
War Diary	Trenches (Henin).	02/04/1917	07/04/1917
War Diary	Ficheux.	08/04/1917	09/04/1917

War Diary	Mercatel.	09/04/1917	10/04/1917
War Diary	Nagpur Trench.	10/04/1917	28/04/1917
War Diary	Croisette.	29/04/1917	30/04/1917
Operation(al) Order(s)	Operation Order E2. By Lieut Col To Elstab. M.C. Commanding D.I.G.	22/04/1917	22/04/1917
Miscellaneous	Appendix I to Report on Operation of 16th (S) Bn Manchester Rgt.	12/04/1918	12/04/1918
Miscellaneous	Report on Operation of 16th (S) Bn. Manchester Rgt. Appendix I.	25/04/1917	25/04/1917
Miscellaneous	16th (S) Bn Manchester Regiment. Casualty List. Appendix II.		
Miscellaneous	16th (S) Bn Manchester Regiment. Casualty List Appendix III.		
Heading	War Diary For The Month Of May. 16th (S) Battalion. Manchester Regiment. Volume XIX.		
War Diary	Croisettes.	01/05/1917	02/05/1917
War Diary	Qudeux.	03/05/1917	19/05/1917
War Diary	Croisettes.	20/05/1917	20/05/1917
War Diary	Hestrus.	21/05/1917	21/05/1917
War Diary	Westrehem.	22/05/1917	23/05/1917
War Diary	Guarbecque.	24/05/1917	24/05/1917
War Diary	Lakreule.	25/05/1917	30/05/1917
War Diary	Acquin.	31/05/1917	31/05/1917
Miscellaneous	16th (S) Bn. Manchester Regiment. Honours and Awards Appendix I.		
Heading	War Diary For The Month Of June 16th (S) Battalion. Manchester Regiment. Volume XX.		
War Diary	Acquin.	01/06/1917	05/06/1917
War Diary	Hillehoek.	06/06/1917	08/06/1917
War Diary	Toronto Camp.	09/06/1917	13/06/1917
War Diary	Trenches.	14/06/1917	20/06/1917
War Diary	Ottawa Camp.	21/06/1917	22/06/1917
War Diary	La Panne.	23/06/1917	27/06/1917
War Diary	Ottawa Camp.	28/06/1917	28/06/1917
War Diary	Canal Reserve Camp.	29/06/1917	30/06/1917
Heading	War Diary-Appendix I 16th (S) Bn Manchester Regiment. Honours and Awards. B/17324 L/Cpl Coxon H. Medaille Militaire. Heninel-Cherisy II Corps R.O. 568. 2.6.17.		
Miscellaneous	War Diary-Appendix II 16th (S) Bn Manchester Regiment. Casualties. June 1917.		
Heading	War Diary For The Month Of July 16th (S) Battalion, Manchester Regiment Volume XXI.		
War Diary	Canal Reserve Camp.	01/07/1917	05/07/1917
War Diary	Zutkerque	06/07/1917	16/07/1917
War Diary	Wippenhoek	17/07/1917	17/07/1917
War Diary	Connavlnt Camp.	18/07/1917	21/07/1917
War Diary	Palace Camp.	22/07/1917	22/07/1917
War Diary	Chateau Segard.	23/07/1917	27/07/1917
War Diary	Zillebeke Bund.	27/07/1917	31/07/1917
Operation(al) Order(s)	Operation Order No. 3. Appendix I.		
Miscellaneous	Amendments to O.O. No. 3.		
Miscellaneous	16th (S) Bn Manchester Regiment Report On Operations (31.7.17) Appendix II.	31/07/1917	31/07/1917
Miscellaneous	A large number of men under the command of Captain orr (Babble) reached the area lying around J.13.b.14.		

Miscellaneous	16th (S) Bn Manchester Regiment. Casualty List. Belgium. Appendix III.		
Miscellaneous	War Diary Appendix IV Awards for month of July 1917.		
Heading	War Diary For The Month Of August 16th (S) Battalion, Manchester Regiment. Volume XXII.		
War Diary	Chateau Segard.	01/08/1917	01/08/1917
War Diary	Dickebusch.	02/08/1917	02/08/1917
War Diary	Wippenhoek.	03/08/1917	03/08/1917
War Diary	Eecke.	04/08/1917	06/08/1917
War Diary	Courte-Croix.	07/08/1917	09/08/1917
War Diary	Berthen.	10/08/1917	21/08/1917
War Diary	Kemmel.	22/08/1917	27/08/1917
War Diary	Messines.	28/08/1917	28/08/1917
War Diary	Trenches.	29/08/1917	31/08/1917
Miscellaneous	List Of Casualties August 1917 Messines, Belgium. Appendix I.	00/08/1917	00/08/1917
Miscellaneous	Casualty List For July. Corrections. Appendix III.		
Heading	War Diary For The Month Of September 16th Battalion Manchester Regiment. Volume XXIII.		
War Diary	Trenches.	01/09/1917	11/09/1917
War Diary	Wytschaete	12/09/1917	19/09/1917
War Diary	Trenches.	20/09/1917	27/09/1917
War Diary	Emmglhill Camp.	30/09/1917	30/09/1917
Miscellaneous	16th (S) Bn Manchester Regiment. Casualties. Belgium. Appendix I.		
Miscellaneous	16th Bn. Manchester Regiment. List of Honours and Awards For August 1917. Appendix II.		
Heading	A War Diary. 16th Bn Manchester Regiment. Volume XXIV October 1917.		
War Diary	Kemmel Hill Camp.	11/09/1917	11/09/1917
War Diary	Wytschaete.	11/09/1917	16/09/1917
War Diary	Trenches.	16/09/1917	20/09/1917
War Diary	Daylight Corner Camp.	20/09/1917	29/09/1917
Miscellaneous	16th Bn Manchester Regiment. Appendix I.	00/10/1917	00/10/1917
Heading	War Diary November 1917 16th Battalion Manchester Regiment. Volume XXV.		
War Diary		07/11/1917	30/11/1917
Miscellaneous	Casualties. November 1917 War Diary Appendix 1.	00/11/1917	00/11/1917
Heading	War Diary For The Month Of December 16th Battalion, Manchester Regiment Volume XXVI.		
War Diary	Torr Top Tunnels.	01/12/1917	02/12/1917
War Diary	Alberta Camp.	03/12/1917	11/12/1917
War Diary	Trenches.	12/12/1917	14/12/1917
War Diary	Stirling Castle.	15/12/1917	15/12/1917
War Diary	Swan Chateau.	18/12/1917	24/12/1917
War Diary	Stirling Castle.	24/12/1917	24/12/1917
War Diary	Trenches.	27/12/1917	27/12/1917
War Diary	Chippewa Camp.	30/12/1917	31/12/1917
Miscellaneous	16th Bn Manchester Regiment. Appendix I.	00/12/1917	00/12/1917
Miscellaneous	Casualties. Belgium. December 1917 War Diary-December 1917 Appendix II.	00/12/1917	00/12/1917
Heading	War Diary For The Month Of January. 16th (S) Battalion Manchester Regiment. Volume XXVII.		
War Diary	Chippewa Camp.	01/01/1918	04/01/1918
War Diary	Lynde.	05/01/1918	05/01/1918

War Diary	La Neuville.	07/01/1918	12/01/1918
War Diary	Vauvillers.	13/01/1918	13/01/1918
War Diary	Nesle.	14/01/1918	18/01/1918
War Diary	Esmery-Hallon.	19/01/1918	25/01/1918
War Diary	Salency Sinceny.	26/01/1918	28/01/1918
Miscellaneous	16th. Battalion Manchester Regiment. Honours And Awards. Appendix 1.	01/02/1918	01/02/1918
Miscellaneous	16th. Battalion Manchester Regiment. Appendix 11.	31/01/1918	31/01/1918
Heading	War Diary For The Month Of February 16th (S) Bn Manchester Regiment. Volume XXVIII.		
War Diary	Les Buttes De Rouby.	01/02/1918	07/02/1918
War Diary	Manicamp.	08/02/1918	08/02/1918
War Diary	Quesmy.	10/02/1918	10/02/1918
War Diary	Ognolles.	11/02/1918	15/02/1918
War Diary	Ham.	20/02/1918	20/02/1918
War Diary	Etreillers.	22/02/1918	28/02/1918
Miscellaneous	16th (S) Bn Manchester Regiment. Honours And Awards. Appendix I.	28/02/1918	28/02/1918
Miscellaneous	16th Bn. Manchester Regiment Appendix II.		
Heading	90th Inf. Bde. 30th Div. War Diary 16th Battn. The Manchester Regiment. March 1918 Attached: Appendices I, II & III.		
Heading	War Diary For The Month of March 1918. 16th (S) Battalion Manchester Regiment. Volume XXIX.		
Miscellaneous	Daily Orders. Part II.		
War Diary	In The Field.	01/03/1918	05/03/1918
War Diary	Etreillers.	05/03/1918	05/03/1918
War Diary	Front Of St Quentin.	05/03/1918	31/03/1918
Heading	Appendices I, II and III.		
Miscellaneous	16th Bn Manchester Regiment. Casualty Report in accordance with 90th Bde 022. Appendix 1.	01/04/1918	01/04/1918
Miscellaneous	16th Bn Manchester Regiment. Honours and Awards. Appendix 11.	01/04/1918	01/04/1918
Miscellaneous	To, G.O.C. 90 Brigade. War Diary March 1918 Appendix III.	02/04/1918	02/04/1918
Heading	War Diary of 16th Bn. Manchester Regt. for month of April 1918. Vol 30.		
Heading	War Diary for the Month of April 1918. 16th (S) Battalion Manchester Regiment. Volume XXX.		
War Diary	Feuquieres.	05/04/1918	05/04/1918
War Diary	Kempton Park.	07/04/1918	07/04/1918
War Diary	Gournier Farm.	12/04/1918	16/04/1918
War Diary	Moulon Camp.	17/04/1918	17/04/1918
War Diary	St. Lawrence Camp.	18/04/1918	18/04/1918
War Diary	Spoil Bank.	19/04/1918	26/04/1918
War Diary	Scottish Camp.	27/04/1918	29/04/1918
Miscellaneous	Ref. Your B.M. 110 d/28.4.18.	28/04/1918	28/04/1918
Miscellaneous	E 313.	01/05/1918	01/05/1918
Miscellaneous	War Diary 16th Bn Manchester Regiment. Honours & Awards Appendix 11.		
Miscellaneous	War Diary. 16th Bn Manchester Regt. Appendix III.		
Heading	16th Manchester Regt. May 1918.		
Heading	War Diary For the month of May, 1918, 16th (S) Battalion Manchester Regiment. Volume XXXI.		
War Diary	Steenvoorde.	02/05/1918	02/05/1918
War Diary	Buyscheere.	03/05/1918	14/05/1918

War Diary	Monthieres.	15/05/1918	16/05/1918
War Diary	Monchaux.	17/05/1918	17/05/1918
Miscellaneous	War Diary. 16th Manchester Regiment. Honours & Awards. Appendix I.		
Miscellaneous	War Diary. 16th Manchester Regiment Appendix II.		
Heading	90th Brigade 30th Division. Battalion was transferred to 14th Division 16.6.18 War Diary 16th Manchester Regt. From 1-6-18 To 30-6-18 Volume No. 32.		
War Diary	Monchaux.	08/06/1918	11/06/1918
War Diary	Bazinval.	12/06/1918	12/06/1918
War Diary	Gamaches.	15/06/1918	15/06/1918
War Diary	Boulogne.	16/06/1918	16/06/1918
War Diary	Cowshot Camp Brookwood.	17/06/1918	17/06/1918
Miscellaneous	16th Bn Manchester Regiment. Honours & Awards. Appendix 1.		

WO95/23391

30TH DIVISION
90TH INFY BDE

16TH BN MANCHESTER REGT
NOV 1915 - JUN 1916

To 14 Div, 42 Bde

SUBJECT: WAR DIARY.

From
    Officer Commanding,
        16th (S) Bn. Manchester Regiment.

To
  Officer i/c A.Gs Office,
      BASE.

      Attached is War Diary complete up to 30th November, 1915, vide F.S. Regulations, Part 11, para. 140, (2).

                                                  Lieut-Col.
              Commanding 16th (S) Bn. Manchester Regiment.

30th November, 1915.

16th Manchesters
Fol: I

12/7635

30th Kivain

Nov. 15
|
June 16

Army Form C. 2118

WAR DIARY
or
INTELLIGENCE SUMMARY G.P.S.
(Erase heading not required.)

Instructions regarding War Diaries and Intelligence Summaries are contained in F.S. Regs., Part II. and the Staff Manual respectively. Title Pages will be prepared in manuscript.

Place	Date	Hour	Summary of Events and Information	Remarks and references to Appendices
LARKHILL	6.11.15	5:30 A.M.	Battalion marched off to entrain at AMESBURY STATION for FOLKESTONE	88
"	7.11.15	2 AM	Transport & details marched off to entrain at AMESBURY STATION for SOUTHAMPTON	90
BOULOGNE	8.11.15	4 pm	Battalion arrived at BOULOGNE & proceeded to camp at OSTROVE	91
"	9.11.15	7 pm	" marched from BOULOGNE, entrained at GARE CENTRALE	92
"	"	"	" arrived at PONTREMY at 12.30 AM 10.11.15	92
ST. RIQUIER	10.11.15	3:45 A.M.	" arriving at ST. RIQUIER. Guides went at PONTREMY so the march was done without him. Much rain & thunder. On arrival billets hastily arranged by town.s. March from PONT REMY much hampered by extra kit carried by the men. Three motor lorries at disposal of B⁴. Lieut Marshall sent on as no information available as to immediate movements of B⁴. difficulty of establishing H.Q. 2C. Transport details arrived here being arrived however day & 1 man left at HARVE with 3 marked tugs	X/9
"	11.11.15		Lt. DAVIDSON & S/Sgt BROWN arrived from HARVE. Lt. BEHRENS & 3/O.R. transferred to BDE trench Coy. L: BEHRENS to command. Training in precincts of billets	89
"	12.11.15		Rev: BALLEIN C. of E. attached to B⁴ Training in precincts of billets	88
"	13.11.15		B² Route—march	89
"	14.11.15	3 pm	C. of E. parade in Square. Funt	89
"	15.11.15	9 am	BDE Route march ; B⁴ first wing from by for training purposes, two slight casualties	89
"	16.11.15		Frost & Snow. Practice loading vehicles.	93

Army Form C. 2118

WAR DIARY
or
INTELLIGENCE SUMMARY

(Erase heading not required.)

Instructions regarding War Diaries and Intelligence Summaries are contained in F.S. Regs., Part II. and the Staff Manual respectively. Title Pages will be prepared in manuscript.

Place	Date	Hour	Summary of Events and Information	Remarks and references to Appendices
BRUCAMPS	17.11.15	4.30pm 12 noon	Arrived at BRUCAMPS & went into billets. Frost. Time taken 1912 am — 12 noon	SA
VILLERS BOCAGE	18.11.15	2 p.m	Arrived at VILLERS BOCAGE marching via SOUEN - FLESSELLES & went into billets. Much difficulty in getting transport out of & of hill at BRUCAMPS owing to horse hoofs not being roughed. Got all heavy draught horse's noughts by smithy at BRUCAMPS who had nails. Transfer rejoining B" at 6 p.m. Half Sacs Ration used by D" Trans. Rations 7.45 & 12.20 P.M.	SA
"	19.11.15		Training in precincts of billets by coys	SA
"	20.11.15		" " " " " by coys. Second Gas Helmet issued (Tube helm)	SA
"	21.11.15		" " " " Visited by chemical advisor 3rd Army. Gas lecture & 13 passes through room full of poison Gas	SA
"	22.11.15		Training in precincts of billets by coys	SA
"	23.11.15		" " " "	SA
"	24.11.15		Bde Route march	SA
"	25.11.15		Training in precincts of billets by coys	SA
"	26.11.15		" " " "	SA
"	27.11.15		" " " " Operation order No 1 attached issued for move into next billet area making a	SA
"	28.11.15		Arrived in fresh billets at BONNEVILLE. Prom Bde Canadian coy disbanded & L/Behrens & men less 2 recruits rejoined the Battalion	SA
BONNEVILLE	29.11.15	12.45 P.M	Training in precincts of Billets	SA
"	30.11.15		" " " "	SA

'a' 16th M/R OPERATION ORDER No. 1.

Ref. Map. AMIENS Sheet 12.   27.11.15.

No 12

1. The Bn. will move into fresh billets to-morrow at FONTVILLE marching by via FIENCELLES - HAVERNAS - CANAPLES.

2. <u>Starting Point & Time of Starting</u> will be Point 130 at 9.15 a.m.

3. Parade on the VILLERS BOCAGE - TAIMAS ROAD in column of route at 9.5 a.m. in order as detailed below.
   Head of Column to be at Cross Roads at Point 130.
   Order of March:- Scouts, Signallers, Sanitary Squad, H.Q.,
   "B" Coy, Quarter Guard, "C" Coy, Band,
   "D" Coy, "A" Coy, Machine Gun Section,
   Transport, Orderly Officer.

4. All blankets will be ready for loading up by Coys as per R.O. No. 7 of yesterday's date at 7 a.m.

5. Capt. Payne, Lieut. Mead, 5 other ranks forming billeting party left here at 11 a.m. to-day.

6. Bde H.Q. will open at Road Junction 300 yards S.W. of C in CANAPLES at 11.30 am.

7. The remainder of day's ration for 28th will be carried in cookers. The supply wagons will carry blankets and on arrival at fresh billets will proceed under the Q.M. to re-filling point, arriving there at 3 p.m. and draw rations for 29th instant. Supply wagons will proceed to re-filling point at 10 a.m. on 29th instant for Rations for 30th instant, from which date re-filling will take place at that time.

8. Re-filling point for 90th Bde will be at CANAPLES.

E G Sotham Capt. & Adjt.
16th (S) Bn. Manchester Regt.

Issued by Orderly at 3.30

No. 1. Copy to O.C. "A".
   "   "   "B".
   "   "   "C".
   "   "   "D".
   "   Scouts.
   "   Signals.
   "   Machine Gun Section.
   "   Transport Section.
   "   Quartermaster.
   "   M.O.
   "   File.
   "   War Diary.

WAR DIARY
16th (S) Bn Manchester Regt (1st City)
INTELLIGENCE SUMMARY
(Erase heading not required.)

Army Form C. 2118

Place	Date	Hour	Summary of Events and Information	Remarks and references to Appendices
BONNEVILLE	Dec 1st 1915		Training in precincts of billets	SS
	2nd		" " " " "	SS
	3rd		" " " A + B Coy musketry on 30 yds Range	SS
	4th		" " " " Machine Gun section machine " "	SS
	5th		Church Parade. Party detailed of 2 L/S + 50 O.Ranks to remain behind for next Machine Gun section parachute on 30 x Range.	
	6th		No 1 + 3 Grenades under Lt Behrens – Bombing practice with machine gun section parachute on 30 x Range.	w.B.
	7th		Battalion (less 1 Officer [2Lt Allen] + 50) Other Ranks marched at 7.40 am to COUIN (15th hrs). See Operation Order No 3 – " Ex conducted into a tent camp in COUIN Chateau park by a S.O. of the 145th Bde. Forward Party – Major Knipe, Kerschaw, Moyse + 2/Lts	
	8th		Moved off 3 companies at 8.30 am at 1/2 hour intervals for on SAILLY (3 miles) when Companies were led by Guides of 144th Bde to LARREY Trench a front of HEBUTERNE 1440th Bde by LARREY Trench a front of HEBUTERNE. The Cross roads in HEBUTERNE village shelled on arrival and	wS.

WAR DIARY
INTELLIGENCE SUMMARY

1/1st 1/5th Gloucestershire Regt. (1st Army)

Place	Date	Hour	Summary of Events and Information	Remarks and references to Appendices
HEBUTERNE	8th		Lt Behrens (severely injured) Lt Mead (slightly) wounded hit. Companies attached for instruction to battalions of the 144th & 8th Brig. as follows —	
			Headquarters to A Company. 4th Gloucestershire Rgt.	
			B Company " 6th " "	
			C " " 7th Worcestershire "	
			D " " 6th " "	
			" Communication section " 7th " "	
			" " " " 6th " "	
			" Machine Gun " " 4th Gloucestershire "	
			" " " " 6th " "	
			During the day HEBUTERNE was shelled heavily and the Battalion suffered 8 Casualties — Most of these would have been avoided if instructions had been issued to Companies of the battalions to which they were attached to inform the men to take cover during the period of bombardment.	G.S.

WAR DIARY
1/5 P.SR Warchester Reg.t (1/2 Brig)
INTELLIGENCE SUMMARY
(Erase heading not required.)

Army Form C. 2118

Place	Date	Hour	Summary of Events and Information	Remarks and references to Appendices
Hebuterne	Dec. 9th		Companies (his Pelotons in 1st line and two pelotons in support unrelieved) occupy trenches. Enemy staff some 15 shells in rear of trenches 5.2 hours in rear - Progress made 27th	A.G.
"	10th		Worcesters Brigaded - Section of front line taken over by but - one Gloucesters by night - 7 p. temporary works - most of the dug-outs have become unserviceable	A.G.
"	11th		Inspected lines of the 6th Gloucesters by day - Trench mortars in "freedom" firing rounds into Gommecourt wood -	A.G.
"	12th		Inspected lines of the 4th & 6th Gloucesters. Water in trenches but much in rear	A.G.
"	13th		Companies take over section of the trenches - Report that line trenches of the Worcesters by night - Moonlight & easier movement	A.G.
"	14th		Reliefs for trenches carried out by 5 a.m. By 6.0 a.m. Coys were very independently and clear of Hebuterne and move by routes Larrey and Jena - D. Company of St Leger and remainder of battalion to Lourencourt. (Billets)	A.G.
Bonneville	16th		Move at 10 a.m. via Beauquesne to Bonneville. Very much and bitterly cold wind. Major Genl Fanshawe 46th Division inspects on march.	A.G.
	17th		Rest of billets - Dr. Senl Stevenson visits at 11 a.m. Lt Allen same Ept-f Resp of Rendezvous diagnosis Rifle & Bn Helmet inspection and inspection of work done in point bring Lithanon, Lewis Eqpt and washing accommodation.	A.G.

Army Form C. 2118

WAR DIARY
1/6th F.F.P. Manchester Rgt ("Coy")
INTELLIGENCE SUMMARY
(Erase heading not required.)

Instructions regarding War Diaries and Intelligence Summaries are contained in F.S. Regs., Part II. and the Staff Manual respectively. Title Pages will be prepared in manuscript.

Place	Date	Hour	Summary of Events and Information	Remarks and references to Appendices
BONNEVILLE	December 1/15			
	18th		Training in billets. Commenced work on improvement of billets.	App.
	19th		Church parade.	app.
	20th		Training in pioneer of billets.	app.
	21st		do	app.
	22nd		Coys Inspn. – Training in pioneer of billets – Major Kempson 2nd in Rhodes evacuated to England	app.
	23rd		do	app.
	24th		do	app.
	25th		Xmas Day. Fire broke out at 12.30 a.m. in 5 fm building occupied by the small detachment of D Company. Fire under control by 6 a.m. – Lieut. Hallam hospitalised	app.
	26th		Church Parade.	app.
	27th		Coys Inspn – Training in musketry. Construction of trenches	app.
	28th		Training in musketry. Trench work.	app.
	29th		do – to RE. Instructed at Divisional Bureau at STOUEN	app.
	30th		do – " " " "	app.
	31st		Training in Trench attack.	app.

Signed E. J. Kerr A.R.
Army H.Q.S. 6th Manchester Regt.

16th MANCHESTER REGIMENT - OPERATION ORDERS No. 2.
by Lieut. Col. Petrie. D.S.O.

1. The Battalion will move into Billets 7th inst. at COUIN for training in Trench Warfare.

2. Advanced Guard,
    Lt. Davidson
    2 Platoons "C" Coy.
    Bn Scouts
    Main body
    Signallers
    Sanitary Squad
    H.Q.
    "C" Coy.
    Q. Guard.
    "D" Coy.
    Band.
    "A" Coy.
    "B" Coy.
    M.Gun Section.
    Transport Section.
    Echelon "A"
    "   "B"
    Train
    Sgt Major
    B.O.O.
    17th Bn.

    The Bn. (order of march as per margin) will march via BEAUQUESNE - MARIEUX - AUTHIEL will be formed up on the BONNEVILLE - VALHEUREUX Road at 7-25 a.m with the head of the main body at starting point.

3. The Starting Point will be the road fork on the BONNEVILLE - VALHEUREUX Road N. of the O. in BONNEVILLE.

4. 2Lt. J. G. Percy will act as Assistant Transport Officer during this march. He will be mounted and his special duty will be to assist in seeing that march discipline is strictly adhered to by the Transport Section.

5. The O.C. Transport Section will detail one N.C.O. to report to O.C. H.Q. Coy Div. Train at BERNEUIL at 11.a.m. on the 6th inst. to take over 4 additional G.S. Wagons for the conveyance of Blankets on this march. These wagons will remain with the Bn. until its return to the 30th DIVISIONAL AREA, when they will at once be returned.

6. On arrival in the new area, rations will be drawn from the 42th DIV. under arrangements which will be communicated later.

7. Blankets will be ready for loading up by Coys in one place for each Coy at 5.30 a.m. Officers Kits on the road near the pond in centre of town at 6 a.m. The Q.M. will arrange to load up as much extra baggage from his stores on the evening of the 6th inst. as possible.

8. A Billeting party under Capt. Elstob comprised of Coy Q M.S. from each Coy, and 1 representative from Transport Section will leave at 8-30 A.M. 6th inst. for COUIN.

                                        Capt & Adjt.
                        16th (S) Bn. MANCHESTER REGIMENT.

Copies issued by Orderly at ..... p.m.
    No. 1   A. Coy.
    No. 2   "B" Coy.
    No. 3   "C" Coy.
    No. 4   "D" Coy.
    No. 5   O.C. Transport.
    No. 6   O.C. Machine Gun.
    No. 7   O.C. Scouts.
    No. 8   Medical Officer.
    No. 9   Quartermaster.
    No. 10   O.C. Signallers.
    No. 11   2nd Lt. Percy.
    No. 12   War Diary (2).
    No. 13   File.
    No. 14   Sergt Major.

16th MANCHESTER REGIMENT - OPERATION ORDER No. 3.
by Lieut-Col. Petrie, D.S.O.   6-12-15.

1. Para. No. 2 Operation Orders No. 2 is hereby cancelled and the following is substituted in its place:-

Advanced Guard.	The Bn. (order of march as per margin) will
Lt. Davidson.	march via BEAUQUESNE - MARIEUX - AUTHIEL and
2 Platoons "C" Coy.	will be formed up in the order named on the
Bn. Scouts.	BONNEVILLE - VAL--------- Road at 7.40 a.m.
Main Body.	with the head of the main body at starting
Signallers.	point.
Sanitary Squad.	
H.Q.	
"C" Coy (less 2 platoons).	
Q.Guard.	
"D" Coy.	
Band.	
"A" Coy.	
"B" Coy.	
M.Gun Section.	
Transport Section.	
Echelon "A".	
R.Q.O. & S.M.	
Motor Ambulance.	
17th Bn.	
Echelon "B" (16th Bn.)	
Echelon "B" (17th Bn.)	
Train.	

Capt. Adjt.
16th (S) Bn. Manchester Regt.

Copies issued by Orderly at 2.15 p.m.
No. 1 A Coy.
   2 B Coy.
   3 C Coy.
   4 D Coy.
   5 O.C.Transport.
   6 O.C.Machine Gun.
   7 O.C.Scouts.
   8 Medical Officer.
   9 Quartermaster.
  10 O.C.Signallers.
  11 2nd Lt. Purcy.
  12 War Diary (2)
  13 File.
  14 Sergt. Major.
  15 Lt. Davidson (also No. 15 O.C. No. 2).

OPERATION ORDERS No. 4 By
Lieut-Col. C.L.R.Petrie, D.S.O.,
Commanding 10th (S) Bn. Manchester Regiment.

13.12.15.

1. The Battalion will be withdrawn from the Trenches by 6 a.m., 14th instant, and will leave HEBUTERNE and rendezvous at camp COUIN in the lines as previously occupied.

2. Companies will move independently, moving to SAILLY by Sections at 200 yards distance and from SAILLY to COUIN by platoons at a similar distance. Companies, etc., attached to "J" & "K" Sections will use LARREY and those attached to "G" & "H" Sections, JENA. Guides will be supplied by Units to which Companies & Sections are attached.
O.C.Companies & Sections using the same trench will mutually arrange order of march prior to leaving trenches, and will arrange so as to ensure that the last section is clear of HEBUTERNE at 6.30 a.m.

3. The O.C. rear Company or Section using LARREY is to report the trench all clear to the O.C. BUCKS Battalion at SAILLY.

4. Transport will be loaded under Company and Section arrangements and will be clear of HEBUTERNE by 7.30 a.m.
Detail as to position of wagons for loading up and time of leaving in certain cases attached.
H.Q. will leave by LARREY trench at 8.15 a.m.

E.G.Sotham
Capt. & Adjt.
10th (S) Bn. Manchester Regiment.

Issued by Orderly at 5 p.m.

Copy No. 1 to O.C. A Coy.
2   B
3   C
4   D
5   Q.M.Sergt.
6   O.C. M.G.Section.
7   "   Signals.
8   Sergt-Major.
9   War Diary.
10   File.

ATTACHMENT OF 16th BATT. THE MANCHESTER REGIMENT.
----

1. The 16th Batt. The Manchester Regt. will be attached to Units of the 144th Infantry Brigade, from the morning of the 8th, until the 14th instant, as follows:-

Headquarters & "A" Company.	4th Gloucestershire Regt.
"B" Company.	6th " "
"C" Company.	7th Worcestershire Regt.
"D" Company.	8th " "
½ Communication Section	7th " "
½ " "	8th " "
½ Machine Gun Section	4th Gloucestershire Regt.
½ " " "	6th " "

2. The six days attachment will be divided as follows:-

   First & Second days.

   Each Company to be split up individually among the garrison of Front line and Support trenches, for 24 hours, two platoons one day, and two the next. Each Officer, N.C.O., and man to be taken charge of and instructed in trench duties by an Officer, N.C.O., or man of the 144th Infantry Brigade.

   Third & Fourth days.

   Two platoons of each Company to take over the dispositions of a platoon in the Front line and Support trenches, changing over at the end of 24 hours, under the command of the O.C., Company, 144th Infantry Brigade.

   Fifth day.

   Companies to remain in Battalion reserve.

   Sixth day.

   The whole Company will take over the dispositions of one of the front Companies, but will be under the command of the O.C., Company, 144th Infantry Brigade.

3.   All Companies, or platoons, not under actual trench instruction will be available for working, carrying, and ration parties.

They will also receive instruction, from selected Officers and N.C.O's of the Units to which they are attached, in all details of present-day trench warfare. Particular attention will be paid to Construction, revetting, and upkeep of trenches and breastworks.

Discipline:

    Care of arms and ammunition.

    Sanitation and hygiene in trenches and billets.

    Sniping and patrolling.

    Use of Grenades, and methods of supply.

4.   The Brigade Grenadier Officer will instruct all Officers of the Battalion in the use of Grenades, at 11.30 a.m. daily, commencing on the 9th instant, at the KEEP.

5.   All reliefs will take place at 2.30 p.m. daily.

6.   Medical Officers will deliver a Lecture to all Officers and N.C.O's attached to their Battalion, on health and sanitation, paying particular attention to precautions necessary to combat gas-attacks, and "trench-foot."

7.   Guides will be at SAILLY Church, on the 8th instant, to conduct Companies and details to HEBUTERNE, via Trench LARREY, as follows:-

    4th Gloucestershire Regt. - 10.0. a.m.

    6th Gloucestershire Regt. - 10.30. a.m.

    7th Worcestershire Regt. - 11.0. a.m.

    8th Worcestershire Regt. - 11.30. a.m.

                                              Captain.
                                               Brigade Major.
4/12/15.   144th Infantry Brigade.

16th Macmillan Vol 3

Bot Dw

WAR DIARY
or
INTELLIGENCE SUMMARY
(Erase heading not required.)

1/6th F.Bn Manchester Regt (1st City)

Army Form C. 2118

Place	Date	Hour	Summary of Events and Information	Remarks and references to Appendices
BONNEVILLE	1916 Jan 1st		Billets in BONNEVILLE.	
"	2nd		90th Bde reinforced by 17th & 20th Bns Kings Liverpool Regt & 2nd Bedfords. Ordered to march to relieve the 153rd Division (Gen. B.A.) of the 10th Corps. The 30th Division takes over the line from River SOMME about ECLUSIER to a point about F1 & Q 1/7. The 5th (N.B.R.) Division of the French 3rd Corps to be on our right. 1st Bn Liverpool SOMME. The 15th Bn on our left & will come under orders of the G.O.C. 30th Division when he takes over.	G.S.
"	3rd		Battalion marched at 2 pm for TALMAS (9 miles).	A.S.
"	4th		" at 9 am to LA HOUSSOYE (12 miles)	A.S. cat.
			" at 6 am to ETINEHAM & CHIPILLY (14 & 17 miles respectively)	G.S.
			Very severe march. The men being heavy loaded & many not independent boots.	
MARICOURT	5th		Battalion marched via BRAY and SUZANNE to MARICOURT and took over the MARICOURT defences from 15th Durhams. Relief completed by 10.30 pm.	G.S.
"	6th		Battalion went into trenches occupying 15th Royal Warwicks A.S. B Coy. trenches 19, 20 & 21, C Coy 22, 23 & 24, A Company 25, 26, 27. B Coy in reserve. Fire trenches 20 & 26 can only be relieved overland. The trenches had suffered —	
"	7th		D Company occupied trenches A3 sector — Situation quiet.	cat.
"	8th		Battalion occupied A3 sector.	cat.
"	9th		Relieved in A3 sector by 15th Royal Warwicks. Relief completed by 9 pm. Bn took over MARICOURT defences.	cat.
"			Bn occupied in cleaning trenches of MARICOURT defences, cleaning billets & village.	cat.

Army Form C. 2118

16th (S). 1st Manchester Regt (1st City)

WAR DIARY
or
INTELLIGENCE SUMMARY
(Erase heading not required.)

Place	Date Jan 1916	Hour	Summary of Events and Information	Remarks and references to Appendices
MARICOURT	10th		Took over A3 Sub-Sector from the 15th ROYAL WARWICKS. Relief occupied from 3pm to 7pm. 15th ROYAL WARWICKS leave for SUZANNE en route to follow 5th DIVISION to rest billets.	AS.
"	11th	11 am	Enemy shelled trenches rejoining for 30 minutes. 4 men of the B2 Oxyper party (50mm) were wounded whilst working on 25 Communication Trench.	AS.
"	"	3/pm	Enemy shelled MARICOURT north and despatch to shells on SEMOOZ Street shew to trenches a daily recon. Both ours and enemy aeroplanes active in the forenoon. Enemy had an observation balloon up to the N.E. of MARICOURT.	AS.
"	12th		A man of battalion transport was wounded by a shell in SUZANNE. 17th Manchesters took over Bury showing garden of 17th Manchesters were billeted in the morning. Relief had completed till 10 pm owing to difficulty of moving machine guns etc A3 SUB-SECTOR from battalion. Battalion went into billets in B section SUZANNE.	AS.
"	13th	am 10.26	The enemy began to shell SUZANNE and CURLU at 2pm. Some 40 5.9 H.E. shells fire. The first shell dropped in CENTRE about near the battalion orderly of the 16th MANCH. R. slightly wounding a prisoner who was being disposed of at the time. Shots of the then fell in CENTRE street on WEST STREET. In WEST street we had 12 men wounded chiefly in B Company.	AS.
"	14th		Brig. Genl. STEAVENSON arrived in SUZANNE taking over A1 A2 A3 A4 SUB-SECTORS from Brig. Genl. BALLARD 14th Bde. 4 day relief notificated.	AS.
"	15th		Battalion chiefly employed in cleaning dug-outs in SUZANNE. B Company which was engaged they had moved into. Major KNOX reported as 2nd in Command demolished by the shellfire on the 14th 15th after	AS.
"	16th	3pm	B Pt. moved up to MARICOURT and took over SUB-SECTOR A3 from 17th MANCHESTERS. B2 moved by sections on night of 15th & 16th to relieved army to enemy sniping being active and by the UPPER hand as the enemy were heavily shelling one of our batteries in the valley 300 x N of the SUZANNE-MARICOURT road.	AS.
"	17th		Occupied in cleaning trenches 20 & 26 specially. Enemy put 40 shrapnels into road about 6.30pm.	AS.

Army Form C. 2118

16/2 J. 18th Manchester Reg (1st A.S.)

WAR DIARY
or
INTELLIGENCE SUMMARY
(Erase heading not required.)

Instructions regarding War Diaries and Intelligence Summaries are contained in F. S. Regs., Part II. and the Staff Manual respectively. Title Pages will be prepared in manuscript.

Place	Date	Hour	Summary of Events and Information	Remarks and references to Appendices
MARICOURT	1916 June 18th		A party sent into MARICOURT wood during the day. Q.M. BARRATT rejoined by order on June 20. He had accidentally injured his hand whilst turning wood.	Appx
	19th		Battalion drill & musketry. Considerable artillery activity during the day. Our snipers reported having killed two Germans of a working party.	Appx
		7.30pm	Some of our section of "B" Company fired on 3 Germans working & fuse-raising 3 trees. There was confirmed by the artillery observer.	Appx
		11.45pm		
	20th		Battalion relieved in A.3 sub-sector by 17th Manchesters and proceeded by platoons to billets in SUZANNE arriving at 4pm. Battalion did not hand over KNOWL in CENTRE STREET. Relief started at 9pm but owing to the difficulty of entering the communication trench the last coy did not reach SUZANNE till 10.30pm.	Appx
SUZANNE	21st		2nd Lt FOWLER and BARRY went to G.H.Q. cadet school on appointment. Lt PHILLIPS and 40 men proceeded the battalion from MARICOURT.	Appx
	22nd		Battalion finding 500 men for fatigue in division.	Appx
	23rd			
	24th		B.M. moved to MARICOURT to take over A3 sub-sector at 7pm 11th Manchesters. Bay. Trenches 22, 23 & 24, A.Coy 26, 26 & 27, B.Coy 19, 20 & 21. C.Coy in Reserve. Enemy shelled valley N of SUZANNE-MARICOURT having which the Company were moving up. No casualties.	Appx
	25th		A very quiet day — Batt. mid-day established an working parties to the some extent went in existing. Two enemy observation balloons were up during the day.	Appx
	26th		Heavy Communication bond to C6. Two enemy observation balloons were up during the day. At 9pm R.E. blew in A.Z gallery to enemy front on Shipley-bury own each saw. Very quiet day hardly any firing. Bent in today. [illegible] intensity lost observing head to German front line and fired into German front line. Actively wrested. Lieut General WALTER G.S.O 1	Appx
	27th		Maj.Gen. STEPHENSON came up & inspected D Coy. trenches in the afternoon. Colonel WALTER C.S.O 1 308th Division back & inspect W.L lines of Trenches. 92 LEE killed by a sniper in 20 trench and Pt G.F.CHACE in trench 26. Enemy at 9pm June came up & repulsed gas attack on the 46th Division.	Appx

Army Form C. 2118

16th J. 10th Manch Regt (126 Bgd.)

WAR DIARY
or
INTELLIGENCE SUMMARY
(Erase heading not required.)

Place	Date	Hour	Summary of Events and Information	Remarks and references to Appendices
MARICOURT	1916 June 26th	6.15 am	At 6.15 am a violent german bombardment by artillery opened. Enemy gunfire shattered things and opened on MARICOURT villages. Orders came for the 17th LIVERPOOLS to man the MARICOURT defences and were reinforced later by 1/2 Coy of the 17th MANCHESTERS from SUZANNE.	
		10 am	The artillery bombardment continued til 6 pm and shells were passing out the 2nd of 30 pm. No lachrymatory shells fell in A.3 Dist. in MARICOURT but SUZANNE appeared heavily received a large number. Capt. HUGHES gave 2 off & 2 N.R. ranks was wounded in SUZANNE - we also had 1 man and 7 adv = 8 off artillery were gas- wounded during the day & men not of first rate condition.	
			The two forward Observation officers in our sector. I expected to win to the S.O.S. 2nd Lieut Barnshaw on attacks probable any of the intensity of the artillery fire.	
		2 pm	Four hundred were not- and front at out my slightly damaged.	
		10.30 pm	Our transport came up from SUZANNE at 10.30 pm and amassing the great difficulties a very god performance. They were not there sheltering in the Dart up.	as
	29th		A gas mask come through sent from- an- fort- our- forward from- a considerable unit neat 12 hour of shelter of the ground by lachrymatory shells, the undoubtedly orders came that there would be no relief. News received that PTE FRIZE had been taken coming from the shelter shuffled in SUZANNE.	as
	30th	2 am	A Zeppelin came over in sector away from H. to W. This no doubt being the one that dropped bombs in PARIS. from the French - hardly any shelling - everything very quiet.	as

16A. 1/8th Manchester Regt (1st T.F. Bgd.)

Army Form C. 2118

WAR DIARY
or
INTELLIGENCE SUMMARY
(Erase heading not required.)

Place	Date	Hour	Summary of Events and Information	Remarks and references to Appendices
MARICOURT A3 sub.	1915 Jan 30th	1.6 pm	Morning misty, wind favourable for a German Gas attack. A German battery of 3 men been taken advantage of the mist to work in front, were unsuccessful in locating our position & neither two were seen to pick him up even in the evening. Enemy quiet during the day but in the evening shouted out "CHEER OH FROM 9 YORKS and MANCHESTERS)"	305
	31st	11.30am	Mr. Whalley speared as a German working party observed in the front line opposite on 26 trench.	
			9 Platoon returned to our relief by 17th Manchesters. H'grs and D Coy returned to SUZANNE, C Coy remained in reserve in the trenches and 2 platoons of B Company in the fire trenches – C Coy & remainder of platoons joined MARICOURT defences. We had had in the trenches for 8 days and the battalion had shown the utmost magnificently.	3 S
		2.30 pm	Pte SLATER accidentally killed in trench 26 and great difficulty experienced in getting him out.	4 S 5 S

Colin Weil
Comdy 1/8th P/8th Manchester Regt
1.2.16.

16 P. Manchester Vol: 4

16th P. Bn MANCHESTER REGT (1st CITY)

WAR DIARY. VOL I. FEBRUARY 1916.

A. Scott
Comg 16 P.S.Bn Manch. R.

Army Form C. 2118

WAR DIARY
or
INTELLIGENCE SUMMARY

16th F. 18th Manchester Regt (12th Corps)

(Erase heading not required.)

Instructions regarding War Diaries and Intelligence Summaries are contained in F. S. Regs., Part II. and the Staff Manual respectively. Title Pages will be prepared in manuscript.

Place	Date	Hour	Summary of Events and Information	Remarks and references to Appendices
SUZANNE	1915 1st		Following ship's current ent. D Coy to ROYAL DRAGOONS. A Coy to SUZANNE 2 platoons B to SUZANNE. Owing to me Coy of the 17th Manchester having been taken 2 platoons B to BUZANNE. The relief of A Coy was not complete till 3 am 2nd bay from ROYAL DRAGOON'S WOOD the relief of A Coy was not complete till 3 am 2nd Quiet night but continued bombardment of the trenches experienced by the Germans from the Trench on the S. of the R. SOMME.	AG
	2nd		C Coy relieved 2 platoons MARICOURT defences. Remaining 2 platoons B Coy reign Coy Hd Qrs at SUZANNE. Continued watching shoot on the S. of the R. SOMME Between French & Germans. The whole about very enemy prevent from D Coy's position at ROYAL DRAGOONS. 1 man wounded. (A Cy)	AG AG AG
	3rd		Continued with shoot on the S. of the R. SOMME. L. Cpl. KELLY. CH. Machine gun section killed by a shell at MARICOURT	CG AG
	4th		Some 20 shells fell in SUZANNE about 11.30 am. Artillery shoot on our right continued.	
	5th		2 platoons B Company moved into A.2. Int. Div's Reserves east of Bois and 2 platoons A Coy were relieved by the 2nd BEDFORDS into billets on R. WORK and returned to SUZANNE. All available men employed improving the dug-outs E. of SUZANNE. Pte F. JELLY died of wounds received at CHIPILLY. Pub. 2nd Lt. J. Drysey transferred to 1st A Coy to	AG AG AG AG AG
MARICOURT	6th		Headquarters and A Coy moved out 8pm to relieve 17th MCHRS in A 3 Sub-Section. Very heavy howitzers 25 + 26 + 27. E Coy from MARICOURT defences moved into Bn. Reserve in A 3. Very heavy artillery shoot on front S. of R. SOMME + constant around BOIS DE VACHE. Our gun opposing from positions between BRAY and SUZANNE and ROYAL DRAGOONS. 1 man wounded.	AG
A 3 Sub- Section	7th		Headquarters moved into new dug-out constructed near Reserve by H.Q. in MARICOURT wood in MARICOURT heavily shelled between 1–2 pm. Kate Br. H.Q. in SCHOOL and evacuated to the present NEW trench from F.7.2.6 to detached front out by Br. Suffolks. Work on new headquarters dug-out being rapidly continued	CG

1875 Wt. W593/826 1,000,000 4/15 J.B.C. & A. A.D.S.S./Forms/C. 2118.

WAR DIARY
INTELLIGENCE SUMMARY

16th F.S.Bn 9th Wiltshire Regt (1st Army)

Army Form C. 2118

Place	Date	Hour	Summary of Events and Information	Remarks and references to Appendices
MARICOURT A 3 Sub-Sector	1916 8th Feb		Quiet day. Only a few W/55. large Minns not seen. New dug-out cookhouse commenced. Work on Communication trench to F.T. 25.7.26 continued. New recruit Pvt French have relieved the last bombers at BOIS DE VACHE. 1 man wounded — from sniper unexpectedly quiet.	A.D.
	9th Feb		Slight fall of snow. Very clear atmosphere — 6 barrage balloons up about 3pm to 5pm. Our Battalion snipers inflict apparent losses. 5.F.T. 25 by two Germs — Charles into Fires; No. C/6643 Sergeant LUCKMAN reported shot dead, who was served by relief at SUZANNE in the same day. He was sniped to the 3rd Wilts Sniping Company. Seriel when about to fire on a sniper. Rifle-front. Some mining done in front of centre section — Sniper very quiet. 8pm. Observed the Germans use wire entanglement very similar to ours.	A.D.
	10th Feb		Very quiet day.	A.D.
	11th Feb		Relieved by 17th Bn Mand R. during evening and moved into Divisional Reserve in SUZANNE. H.Q. in PETIT CHATEAU in CENTRE STREET. Heavy rain and walking bad.	A.D.
SUZANNE	12th Feb 13th Feb		Battalion employed in fatigues. SUZANNE heavily shelled last at 3pm, then at 4pm and from 6 to 7pm. Battalion supplied parties carrying 3 killed, L. Cpl ECKERSLEY, PEGLEAVE and PE SENTLEY. & 16 wounded. Also 1 officer from the Regt B.M. (Captain FLETCHER) and L/Cpl A. BALL been permanent in making the Reserve to effective. —	A.D.
	14th Feb		Quiet day. The 3 men killed yesterday buried by Rev BALLEINS in SUZANNE military Cemetery. French sent warning on hyperdermic at night, German N.J SOMME shouted from a German prisoner —	A.D.

WAR DIARY / INTELLIGENCE SUMMARY

Army Form C. 2118

16th F.S.B. A. Manchester Regt (1st City)

Place	Date	Hour	Summary of Events and Information	Remarks and references to Appendices
SUZANNE	1916 July 15		Battalion in Fatigue Duties. Quiet day —	CoP
	16th		Bn relieved 7th Bn Manchester in A & B subsector. This sub sector is re-christened A.1 and extends under the 69th By 18th week headquarters at BRAY. The trenches in a very bad state owing to the bad weather conditions —	CoP
New A.I Sub sector	17th		Bn busily employed clearing trenches of water. Pumps working continuously. No. D17616 Pte R.A.E. killed by sniper in F.T. 21.	CoP
	18th		Relieved the 14th by 1/6 R. Black Watch and actually two companies were out of trenches when relief orders cancelled — As battalion had had a very hard time in past the bad weather. The disappointment was most felt, but all ranks as usual accepted the matter taken with a good grace —	CoP
	19th		Reported on 1/17 th M.GORDON H'rs shown work done - Leave to Officer started —	CoP
	20th		1/F.16 GORDON H'rs met by an Section of BRONFAY FARM and conducted to Sector — Enemy Artillery had over 9mm. both the Eastern relief unimportant att. 1 AM. Tender atts H'rs in EAST STREET and informed S.G.of R.E.	aP
			No. C/652, Pte POLLITT wounded in the 18 Frants. died in the 21th Country clearing station — Duff. 2 men wounded from fire in the 19th mids inspection by C.O. + returns to compression. 2nd Lt FOWLER and 12 men up for trench arms at CHIPILLY.	CoP
SUZANNE	21st			
	22nd		att on trenches — Attack on FRICOURT reported by 7th Division — a few comments by them limited the protestation were not developed and returned at 7 pm. French C.P. of R. MMME were also attached what is so noted but no prisoners evidently drawn out —	CoP

Army Form C. 2118

WAR DIARY
or
INTELLIGENCE SUMMARY
(Erase heading not required.)

16th F.S.B. 1st Manchester Regt - 11th Bgd.

Instructions regarding War Diaries and Intelligence Summaries are contained in F. S. Regs., Part II. and the Staff Manual respectively. Title Pages will be prepared in manuscript.

Place	Date	Hour	Summary of Events and Information	Remarks and references to Appendices
SUZANNE	23rd Feb 16th		2nd relieved 17th Manchesters in Y.3 (sub.22) sub-sector. Snowing hard & bitterly cold. Transport regained the rise W. of SUZANNE with great difficulty.	A.J.
[illegible]	24th		Snowing. Trenches especially communication trenches very bad. Sergt GLENDINNING T/9 D.R. returned from O.R. POPERINGHE.	A.J.
	25th		Heavy snowfall + bitterly cold. A/7348 Pte SOUTHWOOD + 2/6211 Pte BARBER rejd. Relieved by the 17th F.R. & return to SUZANNE. 2nd Lt MILLIAM S. GREEN by rifle Grenades. Killed during the evening. Headquarters in EAST STREET Church.	A.J.
SUZANNE	26th		Bomb practice. All ranks [illegible] the church went to trenches in small batches whenever Relieve 17th F.R. in trenches of Squad R. Pers very cold but Trenches improved. Relief completed 5.15pm. Brig Gen E.STEPHENSON visited the trenches.	A.J.
	27th		N.C. Gts TRUTTERWORTH & Pte MORE carrying from observers shoots.	A.J.
Y.3 Subsector	28th		Trenches very bad condition. D/7097 Pte DOLEMAN killed in PERONNE trench. T. D/7046 Pte BORKE severely wounded when crossing entrance. C/6753 Pte POINTON shot through at CHIPILY. Some important German work observed in PERONNE trench S.E. 2 June 17.	A.J.
	29th		& killed at an enquiry.	

[signature] M.C.
Army 16th F.S. 1st Manch. R.

XXX (90)
16 Manchester
Vol 5

WAR DIARY

Army Form C. 2118

1st E.P. 1st Manchester Regt (1st City)

INTELLIGENCE SUMMARY
(Erase heading not required.)

Place	Date 1915 March	Hour	Summary of Events and Information	Remarks and references to Appendices
Y.3 Sub sect.	1st	11 a.m.	4.5 HOWITZER battery R.G.A. spend on the Hun German trenches in the PERONNE road — Not considerable damage — Relieved by the 1/F.R.S. We had an adequacy of ammunition the state of the trenches during the time. Wire in trenches cannot be determined as the trenches are very vigilant — Open at once on any party showing itself. Casualties — 4 killed, 46 men wounded.	G.S.
SUZANNE	2nd			G.S.
"	3rd	1.30 a.m.	O.C. 1.30 a.m. a patrol out of Lt. Smyth went out to NORTH trench occupied by D Company fell in with 3 men as ten extricated clear. The remainder 10 men escaped with heavy firing. The disgust not made into a section of about was not completed and it is identified of the on Sheet hair can. Scott Rn. NO D/6823 Corpl BROWN 2/6583 & Cpl THOMAS and D/6577 Pte COWELL was the name of the killed. These men were much by valid — L/Cpl THOMAS had gone up the substitute as a vegetable O came out to the trench — Burial in SUZANNE cemetery of St John. Coord next day — Rejoined 17.5 Bn during the evening. n° 3 — Remainder open trench. Very quiet day. Army	
"	4th			G.S.
Y.3 Sub sect.	5th	4 p.m.	Howitzers shelled near enemy work in PERONNE road — D/7386 Pte Keating killed by sniper in dug-out 10 Sep 1st.	Int.
"	6th		Very cold — 3 rifles charred all. 3 have been hit by our snipers — Patrol sent out to secure portion of our German O.P. running from S.W. corner J. Wood —	Int.
"	7th		Very cold. Trenches improved — Rejoined 2/178 Bn during the evening —	G.S.
SUZANNE	8th		Cold — Battalion moved by no fatigue during.	G.S.

Army Form C. 2118

WAR DIARY
16th F.S. 18th Manchester Regt (1st City)
INTELLIGENCE SUMMARY
(Erase heading not required.)

Place	Date March	Hour	Summary of Events and Information	Remarks and references to Appendices
SUZANNE	9th		Reld. Battalion in tatigue duties — Snow in evening —	G.S.
"	10th		Fatigues.	G.S.
"	11th		Sergt. BAILEY + 26 O.R. joined Bn from base — Relieved 17th–18th during evening —	G.S.
Y3 Suh. sect.	12th		Snow — Trenches much improved —	G.S.
"	13th	3.45 am	"Stand to" on road N.E. and forwards for a gas attack. 9pm 2/4th BUFFS arrive to relieve. Finished in rear of their relieving us —	
"	14	4hr 9.30hr	Enemy snipers active in forenoon. 2nd half Almagile Sept 15. Heavy Bombardment of Maricourt for 15 minutes.	K.L.
"	15	7hr	Very fine. Battalion relieved by 17th Manchesters and march to SUZANNE 11.15	to SUZANNE 11.15
SUZANNE	16		Bn on fatigue all day cleaning SUZANNE. 36 pt. shooting.	1/4
"	17	6pm	Bn relieved in SUZANNE by 1st Buffs, and marched to FRISE & BRAY. Two Companies going FRUISSY.	
BRAY	18		Cleaning of Billets which were filthy	
"	19		Platoon training	
"	20		Battalion on fatigue	
	21			
	22			

WAR DIARY or INTELLIGENCE SUMMARY

Army Form C. 2118

16/5 Bn Manchester Regt (1st City)

Place	Date	Hour	Summary of Events and Information	Remarks and references to Appendices
BRAY	23		Bn on Fatigue	
"	24		"	
"	25		"	
"	26		"	
"	27		"	
"	28		The Battalion marched from BRAY to CORBIE	
CORBIE	29	10am	A Coy proceeded to RIEBEMONT leaving 1 platoon at BONNAY	
"	"	7pm	B Coy proceeded to LONGPRE	
"	30		Fatigue	
"	31		Fatigue	

H Knox Hyne
O.C. 16 Manchester Regt

WAR DIARY INTELLIGENCE SUMMARY

Army Form C. 2118

Vol 6 April 1916
16th S. Bn. or Manchester Regt. XXX

16 Munchsh
Vol. 6

Place	Date	Hour	Summary of Events and Information	Remarks and references to Appendices
CORBIE	April 1st		Corps Fatigue.	A.P.
"	2nd		do	A.P.
"	3rd		do	A.P.
"	4th		do	A.P.
"	5th		do	A.P.
"	6th		do	A.P.
"	7th		2nd Lt PRESTWICH reported for duty and posted to B Coy.	A.P.
"	8th		do	A.P.
"	9th		Sunday - Church parade -	A.P.
"	10th		Corps Fatigue.	A.P.
"	11th		do	A.P.
"	12th		do	A.P.
"	13th		Bn. marched to COISY.	A.P.
"	14th		Bn marched to BRÉILLY (8m. west of AMIENS)	A.P.
"	15th		Company Platoon Training.	A.P.
"	16th		Sunday -	A.P.
"	17th		Platoon Training -	A.P.
"	18th		Company "	A.P.
"	19th		do	A.P.
COISY BREILLY	20th		2nd Lt BARBER transferred to 90th Trench Mortar Battery.	A.P.
"	21st		Battalion training. Draft of 11 men joined B Coy.	A.P.
"	22nd		do	A.P.
"	23rd		do	A.P.
"	24th		Sunday. B.Coy Sports and Horseshow Battalion Sports. Draft of 7 + 2 ints. men joined B Coy.	A.P.
"	25th		Pte training. Draft of 19 men joined B Coy.	A.P.
"	26th		do. 2nd Lt HARVEY joined B Coy and one draft of 15 to D Coy	A.P.
"	27th		do	A.P.

Vol 6 April 1916

WAR DIARY
or 1/6th S. Bn Manchester Regt.
INTELLIGENCE SUMMARY

Army Form C. 2118

Instructions regarding War Diaries and Intelligence Summaries are contained in F. S. Regs., Part II. and the Staff Manual respectively. Title Pages will be prepared in manuscript.

(Erase heading not required.)

Place	Date	Hour	Summary of Events and Information	Remarks and references to Appendices
BREILLY	April 1916 28th		Rest day. A.I.44/4 notified. Genl Fry inspected during forenoon march.	Encl 9
"	29th	5am	Bn marched to CORBIE (17 miles). Bn was inspected by Genl FRY. Battalion put in fine appearance. Much comment on —	Encl 9
CORBIE	30th	9.30am	Bn marched 7 miles to BOIS CELESTINS. 2nd Lt MacDonnell (A Coy) SWAIN (B Coy) HANSCOMB (C Coy) joined for duty.	Encl 9

[signature]
Comndg 1/6 S. Bn Manchester Regt.

16. Manchester
30 Vol 7

Army Form C. 2118

WAR DIARY
or
INTELLIGENCE SUMMARY

(Erase heading not required.)

May 1916   1/16 Bn The Manchester Regt.

Place	Date	Hour	Summary of Events and Information	Remarks and references to Appendices
Camp Bois CELESTINS OZANNE Y.29.d.2.2	May 1st		Men bathed in R.SOMME in morning — Shoot at OZANNE by platoons 2.0 to 4 pm — Adj & Capt R.D.J. Hopkin 2.30pm	A.D.
	2nd		Took over trenches from 7th QUEENS. Relief complete 9.20 pm. A.T.B. Co Francais ½	A.D.
			O.C. Coy G.R.M.R. & Sweere —	
	3rd		Q.M.S. HORLEY Pnt 12.11.2. To hospital O.O. 17 CHIPILLY. 6th	A.D.
		5.30pm	Artillery 100% on FT.A.23/3	
		7.30pm	Bde artillery bombardment of A.23/3 and A.23/9 lasting 6 minutes, our done similar to 1st 15 Bde. Enemy retaliated.	
			Parapet considerably damaged. Repairs being made by B.Coy during the night. A.6380. Pte HOUGHTON 15743 Pte RAMSDEN B.3551 Pte RUANS No 3505 Pte HUGHES each killed. + 7 wounded.	
			2nd Lt PERCY out alone patrolling from dusk to dawn. He could very distinctly make out figures manning	
			2nd Lt STANLEY and his patrol in No Man's land. Bdy returned C Coy to Ft. S. A.29/c. A.23/1. A.23/c.	A.D.
do	4th	2am	4 hostile shell fired in MARICOURT Cemetery	
		4pm	Bombardment of P.9 F.R.OHM Street. Battalion ordered to Stand To and warned up till 5.20 am when	
do	5th	1.50am	85 yds wire & trench round Craft Crater — Two platoons from B reserve were moved up to C Coys in the	
			Supporting trenches & then returned at 3.20 am	
		6.15pm	Shops notified level on A.23/3. fired by A.Coy — Enemy represented since patrolled	
		11pm	Leave for Ehren A.62.B Bridge JOHNSTON & 11445 Pte GREATY, A.27444 Pte	85
			MOTTERSHEAD A.6416 Pte PICKERING killed + 8 wounded	
			Heatcote some wounded. Also Capt. FLETCH DSO 2nd Lt	
do	6th	11am	Army report in DEANSGATE + sorties in trenches	P.G.
		4pm	T. R. Wm. R. Hunt to MARICOURT Cemetery at 4pm.	

1875 Wt. W593/826 1,000,000 4/15 J.B.C. & A. A.D.S.S./Forms/C. 2118.

16th Bn Manchester Regt.

WAR DIARY
or
INTELLIGENCE SUMMARY

Army Form C. 2118

May 1916

Place	Date	Hour	Summary of Events and Information	Remarks and references to Appendices
Y 3 9 d b sect	7		Quiet day -	A.O.
	8		Relieved by 18th K.R.R. at 7 p.m. Completed by 11 p.m. Battalion went to SUZANNE	A.O.
SUZANNE	9		Bn bathed - Fatigues carried on with others.	A.O.
"	10		All MORRIS opening from with Colonel	A.O.
"	11	12 nn	2/Lts YATES and FRANK joined. Draft Bomber & I.B. arrived by one of our scouts.	A.O.
"	12	5 pm	Major MONTO & nearly all Bde Majors Sig & Bde Lewis Staff up. G.S.O.2 with the Sub Division	A.O.
	13	1.50 pm	Enemy opened a heavy fire on Y/3, Y/2 and O/f sectors and on the battalion occupying SUZANNE Trench. Retaliated mainly on the 2nd R.S. Fusiliers in A.29/5 and on trenches A.9 3/2 and A.29/1 and the Orfer. The attacks were supported by machine gun rifle fire into the enemy succeeded in capturing altogether 5 prisoners from the 18th Manchester Regt. Two wounded prisoners belonging to the A.5 r.t. Regt were captured 2/Lt W. MACDONNELL and two men & a wiring party of the battalion were wounded. The Batt Casualties on 13th 5 O.R. killed 30 to Chiefly from shellfire.	A.O.
	14		4/Lt HEATHCOTE RANK posted to Battalion for permanent vice FLETCHER. 30/1-3 S.O.O.T. joined the battalion from STAPLES Captain MAJOR proceeded to England on a few days leave.	A.O.
		8pm	Ordered to return to the 17 Bn. Manchesters.	A.O.

May 1915 / 1st Bn. M. Manchester Regt.

WAR DIARY or INTELLIGENCE SUMMARY

Army Form C. 2118

Place	Date May	Hour	Summary of Events and Information	Remarks and references to Appendices
Y3 Intnd.	15		No. 8780 Pte McKENNA killed by M.G. fire whilst going to Zwarteleen BARR wounded. On convalescent return duty in G.B. McKenna's Inf. Pte. was recommended by the C.O. for a reward for gallantry (see attached medal)	A.P.
"	16		Status are constant during the day.	A.P.
"	17		2nd Lt HARVEY to O.C. 50 yards course at CHIPILLY	A.P.
"	18		Orders to begin a scheme to bring up more from PERONNE and S. of PERONNE and Y. Moulin.	A.P.
"	19		Bn. relieved by 18th Manchesters & returned to SUZANNE. Major HIGGINS 17th K.R.R.	A.P. Others to remain instruct
SUZANNE	20		Capt. Capts. WALKER, WORTHINGTON and ELSTON and Major and 4 other ranks. Then 1 for midday party. Continue preparations for the attack which are to take place on the morning of May 21st.	A.P.
"	21	8:30p	Received orders postponing the attack and preparations.	A.P.
"	22 } 23 } 24 }		Supp. P. 25 O.C. arriving from ETAPLES Bn. in fatigues.	A.P.
"	25		18 Nth. are. Y3 Bn. Oct — 2nd Lt FOWLER to O.C. 1 Company left for SUZANNE to him preparations.	A.P.

WAR DIARY
INTELLIGENCE SUMMARY

16.2.S.18th Manchester Regt

Army Form C. 2118

May 1916

Place	Date	Hour	Summary of Events and Information	Remarks and references to Appendices
Y3 Central	26		Snipers claim 'have killed 5' Germans opposite 14.2.4.c-9. Shrapnel shell burst & relief has taken place during morning in trenches N2.9. NNE. Took over trenches a.b.C.d.C. Gar PERONNE, road from Rd. Lt BEDFORD. These will in future be held by 2 & 3 Battalions. The strong position at PERONNE and Canons in Trench MARICOURT Defences.	
"	27			
"	28		G.O.C. 90th Brigade inspected the trenches at 6.30 a.m. All quiet.	
"	29		All quiet in 1/3. Heavy shelling near CARNOY in the evening	
"	30		All quiet. Bright day.	
"	31		All quiet	

R Johns? Lt.Col.
Comdg 16th Manchester Regt.

Army Form C. 2118

16th B.S. Bn Manchester Regt
WAR DIARY
or
INTELLIGENCE SUMMARY
(Erase heading not required.)

June 15/16

Place	Date	Hour	Summary of Events and Information	Remarks and references to Appendices
V3 Redoubt	June 1st	11.50am	Commandant Chevillon 79th French Infantry gives usual briefing	n.G.
		7.15pm	Bn relieved by 71st French Regt and moves to No 1 Camp ETINEHEM	n.G.
Camp ETINEHEM	2nd		Bn at rest	n.S.
	3rd		do	n.G.
	4th		Bn in fatigues	n.G.
	5th		do Sgt. W. Petrie wounded in knee	n.G.
	6th		do	n.G.
	7th		Strength of 36 O. 2 officers other ranks 782	n.G.
	8th		Lord KITCHENER's death (news received)	n.G.
	9th		Officers of the 16th visit 21 Gnd Cobs	n.G.
	10th		Relieve 108th LIVERPOOLS & 21 Sub-sector, relief commenced 6.30pm complete 9am	n.G.
21 Sub Sector	11th		Heavy hand artillery and artillery fire on front. 3 OR hurt and the French is an officer 2 O.R. wounded	n.G.
	12th		Shelling continues. French commentary 148th French Regt visited our lines	n.G.
	13th		Bn relieved by Myr Ksowa Pocham 2nd I. 1 man wounded	n.G.
		11.30pm	Heavy shelling on town. After 15 minutes harassment Coy by 2nd French losses in own effort Christian was to follow - Subsequently of 1170 men found by this batteries or then engaged in fatigues was transferred by any less 2 French 6 Cowinfrest 2nd Lt FOWLER and 30 O.R. were sent to assistance of the working party	n.G.

WAR DIARY
or
INTELLIGENCE SUMMARY

Army Form C. 2118

(Erase heading not required.)

Place	Date	Hour	Summary of Events and Information	Remarks and references to Appendices
Z1 Schah Ins	13"		Numerous enough patrols were sent out on the south + the outposts were constructed — I Field is ordered to the Green 2 the bridge. The cyclists. The Trench line are out on right, were active during the day. S.9. The widenfaults many at Schon of the South - I the evening 4 my 2nd Lt. FOWLER was badly wounded on mounted while on mounted patrol. Telephonic communication was established throughout & our outposts were in Lowy phase with Ypres until 7 am. Mount Scherve relieved us at 5 am. The field ? Sep Field was friendly. I then shown Trevshe that French were very keen to fire up on occupied by Lt R. NORRIS was killed while - work on outpost. Mr PHILLIPS being wanted. This Span of work outside the trench is making the rest of the outing party. Trenching very muddy, not improved wit. of ypres. Some billeted in mud tunnel in MARICOURT	
	14"		Quiet day. Stay 410 o B. PRICE relieved 4 Sept ? — 1st relieved by 2nd BEDFORDS and went to BOIS DE TAILLES headquart Cpl. SOTHAM cpt 7 the 8 wounded in dayonlines	a.b.
	15"			a.b.
	16"		entered the hand to MEICOURT when BN entrained for AILLY SUR SOMME	a.b.
	17"		rest from their hundred to LE MEILLE vie PICAVIONY — Battalion 24 in full strength four huts in 2 very secure tent	a.b.

Army Form C. 2118

11/5 5/n WAR DIARY Rgn

INTELLIGENCE SUMMARY
(Erase heading not required.)

Place	Date	Hour	Summary of Events and Information	Remarks and references to Appendices
LE MEILLE	June 18th		18h relief in billets.	
	19th		Bn. training in billets, arriere & stores in front of MONTAUBAN concerns.	a.g.
			the men worked at divisional general stores.	
	20th		Bn. training. General the Army hy. soft 5th D in T 17 c 3 d.	a.g.
			GREEN - 9th Gothe pianos pillboxes at divisional general stores	a.g.
			D7142 9th REOPEN continued.	
	21st		Continued, 18th relief. Bn. Moved back to ORVY.	
			Supply J.J.M. JACKSON (c g3 ^ 1 g o 2. Formed the battalion	a.g.
			18th training continued. 2 sd to FAUX (C g5) formed the others (3)	a.g.
ORVY	22nd			a.g.
	23rd		training	a.g.
	24th		do	a.g.
	25th		do	a.g.
	26th	11am	18h marched to ALLY and entrained to MERICOURT and thence marched	a.g.
		2pm	to ETINEHEM arriving 10pm. Heavy artillery barrage —	
	27th		Preparations for enemy stunts. Heavy artillery action.	
ETINEHEM	28th		do	a.g.
	29th			a.g.
	30th			a.g.

Jut
1916

THE NATIONAL ARCHIVES (TNA): TERMS AND CONDITIONS FOR THE SUPPLY OF COPIES OF RECORDS

Copyright

1. Most public records in TNA are in Crown Copyright
There are no restrictions on the use of copies for non-commercial research or private study. Copies, and copies of those copies, may be made and used for education purposes. This covers both teaching and preparation for teaching and/or examination by either teacher or student. Applications for permission to use copies for publication (including web-site publication), exhibition or broadcast or any other purpose must be addressed to TNA Image Library, The National Archives, Kew, Richmond, Surrey TW9 4DU. Email: image-library@nationalarchives.gov.uk

2. Copies of Public Records in privately owned (ie not Crown) Copyright
There are no restrictions on the use of copies for non-commercial research, private study or education (as defined above) within the limits set in UK Copyright Law. Applications for permission to use copies for publication (including web-site publication), exhibition or broadcast or any other purpose must be addressed to the current owner(s) of the Copyright in the original document. Anyone wishing to reproduce the material in transcript, translation or facsimile is responsible for identifying the current owner and for obtaining any permission required. An application must also be made to TNA Image Library (address as above) for use of the copy.

3. Copies of non-public records and of published Copyright works held in TNA
These are supplied subject to the customer completing a declaration form and observing the conditions it contains. Any infringement of these conditions may result in legal action. Any use other than for non-commercial research, private study or education, if approved by the copyright owner, may also require the permission of the Image Library.
TNA Copyright Officer will provide further information on request.

Supplying copies

4. Prices quoted on estimates are valid for three months.

5. Orders for copies placed in person at one of TNA's Record Copying counters are accepted on the following conditions:
   a) TNA may cancel the order if the copying process paid for subsequently proves to be unsuitable, e.g. if it may damage the document or fail to produce good copies. If an order is cancelled for such reasons TNA will offer to refund the payment and if feasible will provide an estimate for completing the work by an alternative copying process.
   b) TNA may cancel the order and refund payments if markers are found to be missing, documents are incorrectly marked up, or customers' instructions are unclear.
   c) If the customer's calculation of the number of copies required proves to be an under-estimate TNA will complete the order but will retain the copies until the balance of payment has been received. If it proves to be an overestimate TNA will refund customers where the balance exceeds £3.00 (or £6.00 for overseas customers).

6. TNA will securely package copies supplied by post and will not accept liability in the event of damage or loss in transit. It can, however, arrange insurance cover at an additional cost if customers request it when they place their order. Such cover will usually be provided by a lower rate international recorded delivery unless otherwise requested by the customer.

7. Customers are advised to seek advise from their Internet Service Provider before placing any order for electronic images to be delivered electronically. Customers should note that digital images are supplied in compressed jpeg format via a link to TNA DocumentsOnline site unless specified otherwise and CD images in tif format. A0 images can only be requested on CD-ROM.

8. TNA will normally aim to provide 'research' quality copies, i.e. sufficient to convey written or graphic information in the original document. There can be no guarantee that it will be able to do so or that the copies will be suitable for any other purpose, e.g. if the original documents are of poor quality. Higher quality copies or copies suitable for other purposes can be supplied if requested when placing an order. Customers are advised to discuss their requirements with TNA staff to ensure the most suitable process can be recommended.

9. Image sizes:
   a) Photocopies and digitally scanned images: TNA will normally produce copied images, which are approximately the same size as the originals. Photocopies will normally be printed onto sheets of paper of the appropriate size in the A2 to A3 range (within preservation guidelines and at the discretion of the operator) and charges will be based on the size of the paper. In the case of digitally scanned copies the images will normally be printed onto paper approximately the same size as the original and charges will be based on the size category into which the paper falls (i.e. A0 to A1, A1 to A2, A2 to A3, A3 to A4. TNA can supply images of sheets of paper of different sizes if customers request it when they place their order.
   b) Prints from microfilm: images will normally be printed onto A3 size paper and may be larger or smaller than the original documents.
   c) Photographs or transparencies can be supplied in the specified dimensions. These will normally be required if a copy is for publication. The Image Library provides such images at the rates indicated in the appropriate leaflet.

Deemed Acceptance

10. TNA will display these terms and conditions at all points of sale. Customers will be deemed to have accepted the terms and conditions in completing an order form, submitting a counter order or accepting documents by any means.

RSD'I' drive/PSdev/PSDP/SSP self service copying/Terms and Conditions - 2.7.2003

	2	cms	The National Archives	ins	1	2
Ref:						

Please note that this copy is supplied subject to the National Archives terms and conditions and that your use of it may be subject to copyright restrictions. Further information is given in the 'Terms and Conditions of supply of the National Archives' leaflet displayed at and available from the Record Copying counter.

War Diary

of

16th Bn. Manchester Regt.

for

July 1916.

16th S. Br. Manch Regt. 90/30 to 16 Manchesters
Vol 4 Army Form C.2118
July. Page 1.

WAR DIARY or INTELLIGENCE SUMMARY

Vol 9

Place	Date	Hour	Summary of Events and Information	Remarks and references to Appendices
MONTAUBAN	1/7	7.22am 6am	Attacked MONTAUBAN. Rising to 1st objective announced. Casualties between Battalion HQ & 1.30pm No A. 2.23. Lt Durnet. A.6.2.0.3. Pte Medcroft. Wet march up from Rainer trenches — to new of Pommiers — Then—	
			alarm about 100 prisoners	
		3pm	Battalion assembled in Talbot Junction —	
HAPPY VALLEY	2/3	12md	Battalion withdrawn via WEST AVENUE and Billon wood	
		7am	to Happy Valley where we bivouacked —	
	3/7		Refitting. Lt-Col Petrie A Coy. Lt OLIVER, B Coy. Capt PAYNE	
	4/7		C Coy. Lt DAVIDSON. D Coy. Capt EATON —	
	5/7		Signal officer Lt MERSON. L.G. Sergt ACHESON —	
	6/7			
	7/7			
	8	1.30. 3.0.	Battalion moved from HAPPY VALLEY to ASSEMBLY TRENCHES. Award ASSEMBLY TRENCHES. CAMBRIDGE COPSE	
	9	4.0am	Marched to VALLEY TRENCH — Battalion concentrated in Brigade Reserve and conveying — Carrying for the Brigade all the march	

War Diary / Intelligence Summary

16th (S/L) Nthbd Regt.

July – Page 2.

Place	Date	Hour	Summary of Events and Information	Remarks and references to Appendices
Montauban Area	July 9	2.30 pm	16th that 14th & 17th Mthbds had withdrawn from Trones Wood. Received orders to move in Glatz Redoubt to Sunken Road, Briqueterie from whence Battn was to attack & occupy S & S.W. pord of Trones Wood. 2½ Coys with C.O. started at once via Glatz Redoubt & worked up Sunken Road, the other ½ Coys followed from Glatz Redoubt & Chimney Trench — All this movement under very heavy artillery fire	
		6.40 pm	Battn formed up on Sunken Rd to attack Trones Wood — 2 Coys forming line, 1 in support, ½ in Reserve — 2 mins interval, 10× between lines. Advance carried out under heavy H.E. Shrapnel, H.E. & M.G. fire — Repulsed 2) Advance enabled Battn. to cover barrage without much loss. Hostile M.G. fire severed — Lx1 Flanco. Battn reached line Trones Alley + S.W. edge of Trones Wood — 1 Coy of 17th Mthbd. was found in occupation of S.E. corner of Wood supporting our right flank — Booted up Trones Alley to point S 29 B & 6 — Worked thro front & retired — Standing patrol left up Trones Alley just west of W edge of Wood	

Army Form C. 2118.

WAR DIARY or INTELLIGENCE SUMMARY.

16th (S) Mchst Rgt

(Erase heading not required.)

JULY - PAGE 3.

Place	Date	Hour	Summary of Events and Information	Remarks and references to Appendices
Bois de Trones Area	July			
	9		2nd R.S.F. holding MALTZ HORN TRENCH — Southern border of wood thickly entangled with fallen Trees + strong undergrowth	
		5.0 pm	Situation: H.Q. + Reserve Coy in SUNKEN ROAD — 3 Coys along TRONES ALLEY + S.W. edge of Wood.	
		11.15 pm	Received orders from Brigade to clear TRONES WOOD Northwards before dawn — any urgent success of Operations depends on it — clean up situation by dawn. 3 Coys 16th Mchs — 1 Coy S.A. Inf. ordered to carry this out by vigorous patrolling up the Wood — Wood was so thick that this could not be done till daylight.	
	10	12.50 am	1 Coy S.A. Inf. which was put under orders of O.C. 16th Mchs. left SUNKEN Rd. ward to fill up gap between 16th Mchs Right + 2nd R.S.F. left in MALTZ HORN TRENCH	
		4.0 am	Our Artillery damage placed on N end of WOOD	
		5.0 am	S.A. Coy report Woods clear of Germans — 4 M.G. sent up towards N. end of Wood	
		5.30 am	Germans reoccupied S. portion of Wood, probably cutting off our Coys further up, are still missing	
			Reserve Coy sent up from SUNKEN Rd. to drive Germans back from S. edge of Wood — Cleared S edge of Wood + reoccupied our trenches just outside Wood	

Army Form C. 2118.

WAR DIARY
or
INTELLIGENCE SUMMARY.

16th (S) Bn. M[anchester] Regt.

JULY - PAGE 4.

(Erase heading not required.)

Place	Date	Hour	Summary of Events and Information	Remarks and references to Appendices
BERNAFAY AREA	July 10		contd. Could not occupy N. Edge of Wood owing to Snipers & Bombers. Many attempts made to get into communication with parties believed to be cut off but unable to do so owing to Artillery Barrage - This went on all day being reported to be occupying centre of Wood strongly.	
		5.0 a.m.	Parts of 17th Manchesters arrived - placed under orders of O.C. 16th Manchesters & sent up to reinforce trenches S. of Wood	
		3.0 p.m.	Urgent orders from Bde. to send strong patrols to reopen communication - Bde. to be informed by 4.30	
		5.20 p.m.	Bde. ordered fresh patrols to be sent out	
		6.45 p.m.	Patrols reported Wood clear of Germans except S. & S.W. edge. Reported that 1 Coy. 17th KLR would attack Trones Alley - S.W. corner of Wood at 9.30 p.m. - 16th Manchesters, 17th Manchesters S.A. & to conform to the Artillery Barrage & would be pd. to Wood after the attack.	
		9.0 p.m.		
		9.30 p.m.	Germans sent up Green rockets in Wood - Heavy Barrage of H.E. put on Sunken Rd.	

Army Form C. 2118.

1st (B) Bn Michat Regt

WAR DIARY
or
INTELLIGENCE SUMMARY.

July - Page 5.

Place	Date	Hour	Summary of Events and Information	Remarks and references to Appendices
Bequetaine Red	July 10	10.30pm	Trenches outside S.W. edge of Wood reoccupied by us.	
		10.45pm	Owing to our troops in Wood the attack was withdrawn to Sunken Rd.	
		11.15pm	Received orders to send troops back at once to Trenches outside Wood — There was tried to patrol of 16th & 15th Middx — Strength 14th Middx (100 strong) moved in Sunken Rd — They were sent up to strengthen garrison of Trench at S. corner of Wood.	
	11	2.0am	Orders received to withdraw 16th, 17th & 15th Middx + S.A. Bn to Sunken Rd commencing 3.0am under protection of our artillery barrage + the attacks of 2nd Beds — This was done.	
		Even	Around Mametz trenches The following Officers went into the action July 8 - 10.

H.Q.   A Co.   B Co.   C Co.   D Co.
Lt.Col. C.J.L. Tothie. D.S.O. Lt. J.N.Oliver Capt. J.J.Payne   Lt. N.S.Davidson   Capt. H. Elstob
Capt. Adj. E.G. Sotham   Lt. B.M.E.Baker Lt. Stafford-Badger 2Lt. S.C.Jackson 2Lt. C.A. Harvey.
Signal Officer Lt. R.A. Megson   Lt. E.H.K. Smithers 2Lt. E.N. Venner 2Lt. A.O. Hoskins.
2Lt. T.A.H. Rand   Lt. H.C. Scudamore

O R 545
| |

Army Form C. 2118.

1/4(?) A Milsex Regt

WAR DIARY
or
INTELLIGENCE SUMMARY.

JULY - PAGE 6.

Place	Date	Hour	Summary of Events and Information	Remarks and references to Appendices
	July			
	11		CASUALTIES during the Trenches Hood in the July 5-10	
			Officers. — Killed in actn. Lieut E.H.K. SMITHERS	
			Wounded. Capt J J PAYNE - Lieut N L DAVIDSON, 2LT T A H NASH	
			2Lt G M HARVEY - Capt WELSTED, slightly (on Duty)	
			Missing. 2Lt E N VENNER - 2Lt T M OLIVER (believed wounded)	
			O R Killed - A/6201 CSM ADAMSON, J H. - A/6551 Cpl H DEWHURST -	
			A/6355 Sgt H ATHERTON - A/6326 Pte J CLEGG	
			B/6470 Pte A BRIGGS - B/6150 Pte H DEAN - B/6511 Pte B JOHNSON	
			B/6517 Pte A KIDING	
			C/4400 Pte J WILDE - C/3303 Pte E T HEWITT	
			D/1115 CSM H HANKEY - D/1236 Sgt T H TURNER - D/1504 Pte J BRANAGAN	
			D/1165 Pte RHYDE - D/1217 Pte A WILKINS.	
			Wounded - A Coy 19 - B Coy 22 - C Coy 23 - D Coy 11 - Total - 75	
			Missing - 10 - 21 - 15 - 3 - 49	
	2.30 pm		Moved to Bois Celestine arriving at 3.30 pm	

2353 Wt. W2544/1454 700,000 5/15 D.D. & L. A.D.S.S./Forms/C. 2118.

WAR DIARY or INTELLIGENCE SUMMARY

July - PAGE 4

Place	Date	Hour	Summary of Events and Information	Remarks and references to Appendices
B-GERMAIN	July 12		Raining	
	13		Marched to DAOURS	
DAOURS	14	10:30am	Guard to General Commanding attending everybody to work here – On recent excellence of work the 30th Div to be used to attack again at an early date instead of 8th July N to life line of Trenches	
	15 & 16		Reorganising – Training	
	17	1:30pm	Marched to BOIS CELESTINS arriving at 7:30 pm	
	20	3:00am	Marched to HAPPY VALLEY arriving at 5:0 am – Lt Col Fahie returned to England	
	21		Reorganising Training	
	22		C.O. Lt Col A Coy B Coy C Coy D Coy	
			Major KNOX Lt F.G. Bavin Lt Megson Lt Stafford-Badger Capt Hawkins Capt Elmes
			2nd in Comd Lt G.C. Harriman Lt A. Officer Lt F. Ricardo Leo Wm Ramsay/Macdonnell
			Received orders at 6:15 pm – to move to Manuel Cospicua – The men were warned 6:0 pm & troops bivouacked for the night	
	23		Moved to Assembly Trenches, Cambridge Copse arriving there 11:45 pm	

Army Form C. 2118.

WAR DIARY
or
INTELLIGENCE SUMMARY.

(Erase heading not required.)

JULY PAGE 8

Place	Date	Hour	Summary of Events and Information	Remarks and references to Appendices
CAMBRIDGE COPSE	24	5.0 a.m.	Received orders to take up position N. of old German front line to 10.0 a.m. — There was an artillery duel, enemy firing in VALLEY TRENCH & VALLEY SUPPORT lay to 5 a.m. Patrols sent out at night to reconnoitre ground between TRONES WOOD & GUILLEMONT.	
	25		Remained in VALLEY TRENCH & VALLEY SUPPORT — Patrols again sent out at night to reconnoitre ground between TRONES WOOD & GUILLEMONT.	
	26		Orders received to move back to MANSEL COPSE on relieving & to return to VALLEY TRENCH & SUPPORT by 11.0 p.m. — Bath left at 10.15 a.m.	
	27	5.30 p.m.	Orders received to bivouac in MANSEL COPSE for the night. Remained in MANSEL COPSE.	
	28			
	29	11.0 a.m.	Moved to VALLEY TRENCH & SUPPORT arriving there at 10.50 a.m. E/R VALLEY TRENCH & S. — handed to MANSEL & ASSEMBLY POSITIONS arriving there at 3.50 a.m. July 30th. No report in general see	Appx II

Army Form C. 2118.

WAR DIARY
or
INTELLIGENCE SUMMARY.
(Erase heading not required.)

July Page 9

Place	Date	Hour	Summary of Events and Information	Remarks and references to Appendices
TRONES WOOD	July 31	5 AM	Returned to orders received to re-assemble Battalion in MANSEL COPSE area	
MANSEL COPSE		12 noon	CASUALTIES during operations KILLED Officers 2/Lt F J BRETT Wounded 2/Lt T.C.W. HAYNES 2/Lt G.C. HARTMAN 2/Lt R.E.S. TUCKEY 2/Lt S.O. JACKSON 2/Lt C.A. WILLIAMS (since died of wounds) 17 Missing Capt J.H. HAWKINS 2/Lt H.G. REID O.R. 17 77 3 (see details) 91	

[signature] Major
Commanding 16th (S) The Manchester Regt

16TH (S) BATTALION, MANCHESTER REGIMENT.

Report on GUILLEMONT operations
July 29/31 1916.

Reference:- Trench Map MONTAUBAN.

1. Battalion, less 2 Coys, (A. & D.) plus half section 90th Brigade Machine Gun Coy. left VALLEY TRENCH and VALLEY SUPPORT on night of July 29th at 11 pm. Marching in file via MONTAUBAN VALLEY and road running N. on West side of BERNAFAY WOOD; hence by track running E. by N. to point 200 yards of N. point of TRONES WOOD, and from there S.E. to trench going N.E. from point S24a11 to S24a68 which was used as ASSEMBLY TRENCH, the trenches dug by pioneers that night not been located as our guides had become casualties on their way up.

   A portion of C.Coy. got mixed with the 17th Mchrs. S. of BERNAFAY WOOD and took the wrong direction so failed to reach assembly point. O.C. 2nd R.S.F. was informed of this and asked to get touch with O.C. Support Coys if possible and divert half Coy to Support or Attack.

   In position at 3-45 am 30th July and Battalion H.Q. established in old dug-out at point S.24.a 11.

   Casualties during march 35 O.R.

2. 2 Coys A. & D. left VALLEY TRENCH at 11-30 pm July 29th and march to ASSEMBLY TRENCHES between BERNAFAY WOOD and TRONES WOOD via same route as the Battalion as far as the N.E. of BERNAFAY WOOD then turning S. to assembly point, arriving there at 2-10 am July 30th.

   Casualties during march 1 O.R.

   Heavy shelling was met with on the march a considerable amount of tear shells and new gas shells being used.

3. Zero hour 4-45 am July 30th. Weather - thick mist. Owing to attacking Coys. being in a position some distance behind the allotted assembly point the first wave was ordered to leave the trench at 4-40 am this was done the remainder of attacking Coys following in 2 further waves 75 yards distance between each wave. Owing to a portion of C.Coy having gone with wrong Battalion and to casualties sustained on the march up it was decided to make the attack in three waves only instead of 4. Half section of 90th Bde M.G.Coy and H.Q. Coy. (25 O.R.) was held in reserve to push forward for consolidation of GUILLEMONT.

   On reaching the Railway running through S.24.C & D. the attacking waves left formed in a very steady manner and using the Railway as a left guide pushed on towards GUILLEMONT. On passing through the German wire, which had been well destroyed by our artillery, heavy machine gun and rifle fire was met with from both flanks which were exposed on the left owing to GUILLEMONT STATION still being in the hands of the enemy and on the right owing to touch with 18th Mchrs not being obtained, the heavy mist making it impossible to see more than 50 to 60 yards.

   Position of enemy machine guns GUILLEMONT STATION and the QUARRY at point T.19.c.13.

   Casualties were very heavy the troops eventually being driven back. Small parties were gathered together and reorganised on a line running N. from S.30a 65 and situation reported to O.C. 2nd R.S.F. This report reached Battalion H.Q. at 6-30 am and was subsequently confirmed by an Officer and a few men who returned to H.Q. Bde. H.Q. was informed and the Bn. H.Q. remained at point S.24 a 11.

4. A heavy barrage was put on the N. and N.E. face of TRONES WOOD by the enemy and continued practically without cessation the whole of the day.

5. COMMUNICATIONS The only communication possible was by runner up to 6-30 pm July 30th when a line was established with 2nd R.S.F. This was constantly being broken however, and at 11 pm owing to an increase in the intensity of shelling the wire got broken at so many point that repair became impossible.

16TH (S) BATTALION MANCHESTER REGIMENT.

Report on GUILLEMONT operations
July 29/31 1916.

SHEET NO 2.

6. At 8-10 pm word was received from O.C. Support Coys. that relief would take place the same night and at 5 am July 31st message received that A.Coy and small parties of B. and C. Coys were then being relieved and moving off to MANSEL COPSE.

APPENDIX I

Brief Report of Operations carried out
by 16th Manchester Regiment on July 1st/2nd.
....

(In accordance with Bde. Operation Order No 23.)

July 3rd 1916.

Left Assembly trenches 8-30 am in formation as previously practised. Moved up as close as possible to our artillery barrage and halted about 9-20 am. Maintained communications with the 17th Manchester Regt. on our right, but were under heavy machine gun and rifle fire from our left rear, being unsupported by troops on our left. At 9-55 am on the artillery barrage lifting, no supporting troops still appearing on our left and the hostile machine gun fire still being very severe, the advance could not be continued. At 10-5 am, on the appearance of the leading troops attacking on our left, continued the advance and without a check passed through MONTAUBAN and seized and occupied MONTAUBAN ALLEY at 10-30 am and immediately proceeded to consolidate as follows:- A., B., and C. Companies MONTAUBAN ALLEY; D. Company edge of village also Keeps F. and D., and established H.Q. in Valley trench immediately S. of D. Keep.

About 9-30 pm enemy attacked against our front and left, S.O.S. sent, barrage placed on our right front (a few shells too short), attack held up by M.G. and rifle fire, and eventually withdrawn under cover of darkness.

During night 1st/2nd continual bombardment from E. and N. with heavy shells.

At 3-30 am on the 2nd enemy counter-attacked along the whole front, S.O.S. sent, but no reply for 15 minutes: brought to a standstill along front at 250 yds distance.

Number of attacking troops estimated at two battalions: front attacked about 800 yds.

Enemy entered MONTAUBAN ALLEY on our right and a bombing encounter ensued with our right flank. Asked O.C. MONTAUBAN for support and one company immediately placed at my disposal, and two platoons sent up to reinforce. About 5 am Headquarters and two leading companies 2nd Wilts arrived to relieve. The enemy counter attack having been withdrawn about 4 a.m. having suffered heavily from M.G. L.G. and rifle fire, but their bombing party left in our trenches.

Relief commenced about 8 am. and battalion withdrawn by 1-30 pm.

Captured two guns and 16th Manchester Regt written on them, also names of men who captured them - and about a hundred prisoners.

(Sd) C.L.Petrie, Lt.Col.,
Commanding 16th (S) Bn. Manchester Regiment.

90th Brigade.

30th Division.

1/16th BATTALION

MANCHESTER REGIMENT

AUGUST 1 9 1 6

WAR DIARY or INTELLIGENCE SUMMARY

Army Form C. 2118

AUGUST — Page 1

Place	Date	Hour	Summary of Events and Information	Remarks and references to Appendices
MANSEL COPSE	AUG. 1		Resting in Mansel Copse Area	
	2	3.30 a.m.	Marched to Mericourt entraining there at 12 noon for Longpre which was reached at 6.0 p.m.	
	3		Cleaning up.	
	4		Entrained 9.30 p.m for Berguette which was reached at 6 a.m 5th.	
	5	8.15 am	Marched to Busnes where the Batt. billetted - We are in XI.th Corps, 1st Army.	
	6-9		Training	
	10	3.0 p.m	Inspected by Gen. Sir R.C.B. Haking, 1st Army Commander - Congratulated on Smart turn out of the men.	
	11	5.10 a.m	Marched to billets at Essars, near Bethune, arriving at 9.0 a.m.	
	12-31		Training - During this period various working parties were supplied for various trades.	
	29	3.4 p.m	The Divisional General inspected the billets of the Batt.	
	31	11.15 a.m	Inspection of the Batt. & Transport by the Divisional General. Batt. & Transport turned out very well.	

H.H. Moore Lt Col
Commdg. 16th (S) The Manchester Regt.

VOLUME XI.

SECRET.

WAR DIARY.

FOR THE MONTH OF SEPTEMBER.

16TH BN. MANCHESTER REGIMENT.

H Prior
                                    Lieut-Col.
Commanding 16th (S) Bn. Manchester Regiment.

5.10.1916.

Army Form C. 2118.

WAR DIARY
or
INTELLIGENCE SUMMARY

(Erase heading not required.)

16th M/chrs — SEPTEMBER — Page 1.

Instructions regarding War Diaries and Intelligence Summaries are contained in F.S. Regs., Part II. and the Staff Manual respectively. Title Pages will be prepared in manuscript.

Place	Date	Hour	Summary of Events and Information	Remarks and references to Appendices
ESSARS	Sept. 1-2		Training.	
FESTUBERT	3		Took over Southern section of FESTUBERT trenches from 15th W. Yorks — One Coy SB 11th M/chrs had to this Battn. to make up strength. Dispositions — D Coy on Left — B Coy on Right A Coy Splt between D & B Coy B 11th M/chrs in Support to Left — C Coy in Support to Right The Bn. stuck here for 5 days was very quiet & there were no casualties — Patrols & wiring parties were out nightly. Relieved by 11th M/chrs, leaving one Coy (C) in the line to make up strength.	See APPENDIX I.
	8		—	See APPENDIX II.
			Took over Village Line from 2nd R.S.F. Bn. lasted six days — very quiet.	
	14		Changed places with 14th M/chrs — Dispositions in Trenches same as previous from Sept. 3–8.	See APPENDIX III.
BETHUNE	16		Relieved by 14th E. Lancs & marched to BETHUNE, arriving at 6.30 a.m.	
BUSNETTE	17		Left BETHUNE at 2.0 p.m. & marched to Billets in BUSNETTE, arriving at 6.0 p.m.	
BEAUVAL	17		Left BUSNETTE at 6.0 p.m. & marched to CHOCQUES entraining there for CANDAS & thence marched from there to Billets at BEAUVAL arriving at 3.30 a.m. on the 19th. Arrived from there to Billets at BEAUVAL	

J. Moore Lt. Col.
Comdg. 16th M/chrs Regt.

Army Form C. 2118.

WAR DIARY
or
INTELLIGENCE SUMMARY

14th Afrs - SEPTEMBER - Page 2

(Erase heading not required.)

Place	Date	Hour	Summary of Events and Information	Remarks and references to Appendices
	Sept			
BEAUVAL	19-20		Training	
FLESSELLES	21	9.30am	Arrived & billeted in FLESSELLES arriving unit day	
			Brigade Training	
	22-30		Casualties during the month OR 2 killed & 1 Died of wounds - These casualties occurred during the short tour in FESTUBERT Trenches Sept 12-16.	
			Honours awarded for Operations (July) on the SOMME are as follows:	
			Officers Capt. & P. HEATHCOTE, R.A.M.C. — 2nd 14th Bn. Croix de Guerre.	
			OR 6136 A/Cpl. TSHIE, R. (Russian) → Medal of St George (4th Class) and Military Medal.	
			4035 A/Cpl. PALMER, H.	
			6525 Pte. BAINES, G.	
			6246 " FROOD, C.F.	
			7599 " BOWIE, D.	
			9113 " GREAVES, N	
			6445 " WAYNE, C.A.	
			6365 A/Cpl. DAWSON, S.P.	
			6694 " SHEARD, G.	
			6522 Pte. WORDSWORTH, S.	

H. Moore
Commdg. 14th Afrs. Ret.

16th (S) BN. MANCHESTER REGIMENT

OPERATION ORDERS NUMBER G.4.
-BY-
LIEUT. COL. H. KNOX,
Commanding 16th (S) Battalion Manchester Regiment.

Ref. Sheet 36A. S.E.
36B. N.E.

1. The 16th Bn Manchester Regiment will relieve the 15th W. Yorks. Regiment in the right sector of the FESTUBERT sector on the 3rd Sept.

2. The present billets will be taken over by the 2nd Yorks.

3. Tour of duty will be 4 days.

4. The Battalion will march with a distance of 200^x between Coys. up to N. & S. line drawn between LE TOURET and GORRE CHATEAU. E. of this line the march will be with 50^x distance between platoons.

5. Order of March:- B., A. (less 2 platoons), D., 2 platoons A.Coy., C., H.Q., Coy. of 17th Manchesters.

6. Route:- LE HAMEL - GORRE - and the road running through F.4 a - F.5 a & b to point X 30 c.95.20 where guides will be provided by 15th W.Yorks. Regt.
Guides:- 4 guides will meet B.Coy & A.Coy (less 2 platoons) for the Right front Subsector - they will be numbered 1 to 4.
4 guides will meet D.Coy. and 2 platoons A.Coy for the Left front Subsector - they will be numbered 5 - 8.
2 Guides will meet C.Coy for the right Support O.B.L. - they will be numbered 9 & 10.
2 guides will meet the Coy of 17th Manchesters for Left Support O.B.L. - they will be numbered 11 and 12.

7. The necessity for carrying out the relief as silently as possible must be impressed on all ranks - No smoking from time of leaving ESSARS till relief complete.

8. Special attention will be paid to taking over:
    (a) Keeps and Defensive Posts with Ammunition and Stores correct.
    (b) Snipers and Observation Posts and Rifle Grenade Batteries.
    (c) Defence Schemes, Maps, Aero Photos, Log Books, Intelligence summaries and Statements of work in hand or to be carried out.

9. Completion of reliefs will be reported to Bn H.Q.

10. All trench stores will be taken over from the 93rd B'de and receipt given for them - Duplicate to be forwarded to Bn H.Q. by 8 am 4th instant.

11. The general policy of the 15th W.Yorks. Regt. will be followed & it is most necessary that the enemy should be kept in ignorance of the relief as long as possible.

12. C.Coy will mount a guard of 1 N.C.O. and 3 men at the entrance to Barnton Rd Trench on the FESTUBERT road and report that the present guard is relieved.

13. Lewis Gunners to be at Bn H.Q. in O.B.L. at 2-0 pm 3rd instant. Parade under orders of L.G.O. - Any Reserve Lewis Gunners required to help carrying Guns and magazines will be returned to their Coys when guns are in position and should be posted in support or Reserve positions where possible.

14. Signallers to be at Bn H.Q. in O.B.L. at 2-30 pm 3rd inst. Parade under orders of Signalling officer.

15. 1 Officer and Q.M.Sgt from each Coy to be at Bn H.Q. in O.B.L. at 5-30 pm to take over trench stores.

OPERATION ORDERS NUMBER G.4 (Continued)

15 (cont) A Coy Officer and Q.M.S. will take over the Trench Stores in the Left Support subsector O.B.L. (portion to be occupied by Coy of 17th Manchesters.).
R.S.M. will proceed with this party and take over H.Q. Trench Stores.

16. Usual Billets "Clean" and "No Claim" certificates will be sent in to Orderly Room.

17. Ref. para 5: Head of B.Coy to be level with road leading to Transport at 6-30 pm.

Sept. 2nd 1916.

................Lt & Act Adjt.
16th (S) Bn Manchester Regiment.

WAR DIARY – VOLUME XI
APPENDIX II

OPERATION ORDER NO. G. 5 by
Lt. Col. H. KNOX, Commanding 16th MANCHESTER REGT.
September 7th 1916.

1. The Front Line System of Trenches and the portion of the O.B.L. occupied by H.Q. Coy., of ELSIE will be taken over by KITTY on the night of Sept. 8th.

2. C. Coy will remain in present position in O.B.L.
D. Coy of KITTY will remain in present position in O.B.L.

3. O.C. Right Front Coy will detail 4 Guides; they will be numbered 1 to 4.
O.C. Left Front Coy will detail 4 Guides; they will be numbered 5 to 8.
The R.S.M. will detail 2 Guides for H.Q. Coy. they will be numbered 9 & 10.
All above-mentioned Guides to be at junction of BARNTON RD and FESTUBERT ROAD at 8.30 p.m.
GUIDES TO BE PARTICULARLY NOT TO WALK TOO FAST UP THE TRENCHES.
Particulars of Routes will be settled at the CONFERENCE which will be held at 10 a.m. 8th inst., instead of 10.30.
O's. C. Right and Left Front Coys., to have Guides for each Island at their Coy H.Q. at 9.0 p.m.

4. 2nd. Lt. HENDRIE will remain at Right Front Coy H.Q., and 2nd. Lt. HEYWOOD at Left Front Coy H.Q. for the night of 8/9 after KITTY XXXXXX has taken over and render all possible assistance to the incoming Coy Commander.

———

5. After KITTY has taken over ELSIE XXXXXX (less 1 Coy) will take over the VILLAGE LINE from ADA.

6. Preliminary arrangements for taking over will be as under.
2nd. Lt. HILTON of C. Coy to relieve 2nd. Lt. RYLANDS in the Right Front Sub-sector at 8.30 a.m. on the 8th and remain there until KITTY has taken over when he will return to C. Coy in the O.B.L.
The officers mentioned below will be at H.Q. Mess at 10 a.m (also the N.C.O's) and at ADA's H.Q. at 11.0 a.m. for purpose of arranging the taking over of Posts and Stores.

  A. Coy. 2nd. Lt. RYLANDS 1 N.C.O.
  B. Coy. 2nd. Lt. SMITH.   1 N.C.O.
  D. Coy. 2nd. Lt. WRIGHT   1 N.C.O.
  H.Q. Coy. (Signals) Sgt. PENNINGTON
       (Lewis Guns) Sgt. HOYE.
       (Stores) 1 N.C.O.

2nd. Lt. SMITH will be detailed at H.Q., the R.S.M. will detail N.C.O's from H.Q. Coy. The remainder of Officers and N.C.O's will be detailed by Coy Commanders concerned.

7. 34 men of A. Coy (2 of them from a Lewis Gun Team) will be at Junction of BARNTON ROAD & FESTUBERT ROAD at 1.30 p.m. to take over 17 Posts in Village Line and Stores connected with each – 2 men to go to each Post – 1 Man from each Post to return and meet Coy as it leaves the Trenches, at point to be arranged by O.C. A. Coy., and to be at that point at 9.30 p.m. to guide remainder of Coy to the various Posts.
These 34 men of A. Coy will be drawn from the Right Front Coy sector. O.C. B. Coy to thin out other Posts to allow of these men being withdrawn.
NOTE: THESE MEN MUST BE AT THE END OF BARNTON ROAD AT 1.30 p.m. SHARP.

            Lt. & A/Adj.

War Diary - Volume XI
Appendix III

OPERATION ORDERS NO. G.7
BY LIEUT. COL. H. KNOX,
COMMANDING ELSIE.

Sept. 14th/16.

1. Operations Orders G.6 hereby cancelled.

2. ELSIE will relieve KITTY in Right FESTUBERT Sector on night 14/15 - KITTY at the same time taking over VILLAGE LINE from ELSIE.

3. Distribution of Coys in trenches as before - O's C. B. and D. Coys to report number of men required to make up posts and O.C. A. COY to report number available by 2 pm.

4. The 2 Observers who occupied O.P. near end of BARNTON ROAD to take over that post at 4 pm.

5. ELSIE Lewis Guns will relieve KITTY Lewis Guns at 2-0 pm.
   ELSIE Signals relieve KITTY Signals at 2-30 pm.
   ELSIE Snipers relieve KITTY Snipers at 4-0 pm.

6. 1 N.C.O. per Coy, and 1 N.C.O. for H.Q. to be at KITTY H.Q. at 5pm to take over trench stores, which must be done carefully.

7. Reconnoissance of VILLAGE LINE by KITTY.
   Meeting point - Junction of BARNTON ROAD and FESTUBERT ROAD, 11 am. O.C. A.Coy will arrange to meet Officer of KITTY re scattered posts.
       O.C.B.Coy will arrange to meet Officer and N.C.O. of KITTY re LE PLANTIN.
       O.C.D.Coy will arrange to meet Officer and 2 N.C.O's of KITTY re FESTUBERT and CAILLOUX.
       L.G.O. and 1 guide per team (6) will meet L.G.O. KITTY and 1 man per team (6).
       4 Signallers (1 per station) will meet 4 Signallers of KITTY.
       1 Guide from O.P. in SCHOOL will meet 4 Snipers of KITTY and take them to O.P.

   1-30 pm. A.Coy. 1 man per post, with exception of No 8 the L.G. Post which will be relieved by arrangements of L.G.O., will meet 32 men of KITTY and guide them to the various posts, each post after handing over to close in by 7 pm at point to be arranged by O.C. A.Coy.
   Reference LEWIS GUN POST - The L.G.O. will see that the work of pumping is not interrupted by the relief.

8. All orders for Keeps and Posts and all stores to be carefully handed over and signatures obtained for the latter.

9. As soon as Coys have completed relief in the trenches the following message will be sent "CARVING FORK".

........Lt. & Act Adj
ELSIE.

Copies to:-
4 Coys.
L.G.O.
Signals.
R.S.M.
Sgt. Kelly.
Q.M.
KITTY.

VOLUMN XII.

SECRET.

WAR DIARY.

FOR THE MONTH OF OCTOBER.

16TH BN. MANCHESTER REGIMENT.

3-10-1916.

W Elstob MAJOR,
Commanding 16th (S) Bn. Manchester Regiment.

Army Form C. 2118.

WAR DIARY
INTELLIGENCE SUMMARY
(Erase heading not required.)

Vol XII
16TH S. Bn. MANCHESTER Regt.
OCTOBER — Page 1.

Place	Date	Hour	Summary of Events and Information	Remarks and references to Appendices
FLESSELLES	Oct. 1, 2, 3		Training. Transport moved by road to CARDONETTE	
	4.		Batt. moved by Motor Bus to BUIRÉ — Left Flesselles at 9 a.m. Reached point on VIGNACOURT RD for "Embussing" at 10.15 a.m. "Embussed" at 12.30 p.m. arrived BUIRÉ 5 p.m. Transport moved from CARDONETTE to BUIRÉ by road.	
BUIRÉ	5		Cleaning up & organising	
	6	4.15 p.	Marched to FRICOURT CAMP arriving about 4.30 p.m.	
	7, 8, 9		Training & organising	
	10.	4 a.m.	Marched to field N. of MONTAUBAN where the Batt. fell out still 6 p.m. when the march was continued with intention of occupying FLERS TRENCH & SUPPORT — On reaching LONGUEVAL word was received that there was no room in those trenches so halted and made our ground W. of DELVILLE WOOD & the troops bivouacked for the night.	
TRENCHES.	11.	7.30 a.m.	Marched to FLERS SUPPORT & GROVE ALLEY. — H.Q. in FLERS SUPPORT.	
	12.	5.45 p.	Orders received to move up to reinforce 17th Mchrs in front line & GIRD SUPPORT — This was done, the Batt. (less 1 Platoon of A Coy) being in position by 10.0 p.m. — H.Q. in GIRD TRENCH	The Trenches in this sector being old Boche ones, the SUPPORT Trenches mentioned were the mainside German front line
	13.		GIRD TRENCH & Bn. H.Q. heavily shelled — Lt. Col H Knox killed by shell fire whilst moving H Q Coy further along the Trench to get out of the shelling zone. In the evening Major W EUSTOB took over command of the Battn.	

2449 Wt. W14957/M90 759,000 1/16 J.B.C. & A. Forms/C.2118/12.

WAR DIARY or INTELLIGENCE SUMMARY

Army Form C. 2118.

Vol XII

16TH S. BN. MANCHESTER REGT

OCTOBER — Page 2

Place	Date	Hour	Summary of Events and Information	Remarks and references to Appendices
TRENCHES	Oct. 14.		Orders received to shift H.Q. from GIRD TRENCH. — This was done, a position nearer the front line just off GIRD SUPPORT being chosen.	
	15.		Heavily shelled by Boche at 3·30 a.m. & 5·30 a.m.	
	16.	9·15 a.m.	Orders received	
		11·0 a.m. & 2·15 p.m.	These was done the rations being brought 2,000x being cleared — In the evening the 2nd Yorkshire Regt. took over our position of the line & we moved back to SWITCH TRENCH.	
	17.		In reserve to 21st Bde. — Orders received for 2 Coys. to go up & hold front line whilst 21st B'de attacked on the 17th. — A & D Coys. sent up.	
	18.	6·25	Orders received for Bn. (less 2 Coys.) do shift forward to FLERS TRENCH — A position at F.15	
		4·30 p.m.	Orders received to shift H.Q. & 2 Coys back to SWITCH TRENCH — this was accomplished by 10·30 p.m. Notification that 1 Coy in front line would be relieved & sent back to join the rest of Battn. in SWITCH TRENCH. Both Coys in front line were relieved & arrived in SWITCH TRENCH by 8·0 a.m. 19/10.	
	19.	12·0 noon	Orders to be ready to move to Camps near MONTAUBAN (S.24d) some time in the evening received	
		6·30 p.m.	Definite orders to shift — Left SWITCH TRENCH at 7·30 p.m. arrived MONTAUBAN CAMP at 3·15 a.m. 20/10	
MONTAUBAN CAMP	20. 21.		Resting & cleaning up.	
	22.	7·30 a.m.	Left MONTAUBAN CAMP & marched to billets in RIBEMONT, arriving at 12·30 p.m.	
RIBEMONT	23. 24.		Cleaning up & Training	
	25.	6·0 a.m.	Transport moved by road to TALMAS	
	26.	7·30 a.m.	Batt. moved by Bus to Sus. ST. LEGER which was reached at 5·0 p.m. 3rd Army - VIIth Corps. Transport moved by road from TALMAS to Sus. ST. LEGER	

Army Form C. 2118.

WAR DIARY
or
INTELLIGENCE SUMMARY

Vol XII

16TH (S) Bn. MANCHESTER RGT.

OCTOBER — Page 3.

(Erase heading not required.)

Place	Date	Hour	Summary of Events and Information	Remarks and references to Appendices
SUS. ST. LEGER	Oct. 24		Training	
	28	1.0 a.m.	Left Sus. St. Leger & marched to Billets in Bailleulval arriving at 6.0 pm	
	29.		Relieved 7th Sherwood Foresters in Left Sect. of Blaireville Trenches — Relief complete at 11:30 a.m. Dispositions: Front Line C. Cy. B. ¼ D. 2 Platoons and A Coy. Support " C. Cy. B. ¼ D. 2 " Reserve (in Bretencourt) A. Coy.	
	30. 31.		Very quiet. Hanno awarded during the month Military Medal to 6412 C.S.M. Allen, H. for Trones Wood July 9/16 " " 6235 Pte. A. Deaville for Guillemont July 30th CASUALTIES during the month (all between Oct 17th & 19th). Killed. Died of Wounds. Wounded. Missing. Officers 1 — 2 — (1 slightly at duty) O.R. 20 8 64 1 For details of Casualties see Appendix I (Oct)	APPENDIX I

W.T. Webb, Major
Commanding 16th (S) Bn. M/ch'r Rgt.

16th (S) Battalion Manchester Regiment. *WAR DIARY. APPENDIX I (Oct)*

CASUALTIES OCTOBER 1916.

OFFICERS.

Lt. Colonel H. Knox.	Killed in Action Oct 13th 1916.
Lt. A.F.D. Knight.	Wounded in Action Oct. 11th 1916.
Captain R.H. Megson.	Wounded Slightly at Duty Oct. 15th 1916.

OTHER RANKS
KILLED IN ACTION.

A/6596 Sgt. Corkhill J.R.	Oct. 12th 1916.
B/6660 Sgt. Naylor, H.	-do-
B/6496 L/Cpl. Hadfield, D.D.	-do-
B/6628 Pte. Hill, R.	-do-
B/27047 Pte. Parkinson, F.	-do-
B/43013 " Winstanley, R.	-do-
B/35463 " Boyd, F.H.	-do-
B/27320 " Moore, H.	-do-
C/6777 L/C. McElhinney, J.	Oct. 14th 1916.
C/6714 Pte. Bancroft, J	-do-
C/35496 " Farnsworth, T.	-do-
A/6683 Sgt. Smith, R.	Oct. 15th/1916.
B/35993 Pte. Keegan, A.	-do-
A/43019 L/C Duff, J.	Oct. 18th/19th 1916
A/6400 " Littler, J.L.	-do-
C/35804 Pte. Little, W.	-do-
C/7274 " Wilson, R.	-do-
C/35566 " Stafford, F.R.	-do-
C/40894 " Bagley, E.E.	-do-
D/43058 Cpl. Oates, B.	-do-

DIED OF WOUNDS.

B/32942 Pte. Hilton, R	Oct 12th 1916.
B/43015 Pte. Lait, C.	Oct 13th 1916.
C/6766 Pte. Jones, R.V.	Oct 15th 1916.
C/6998 Pte. Knowles, A.	-do-
A/6524 Cpl. Martin, F.	-do-
C/40914 Pte. Gould, H.	Oct 13th 1916.
D/6443 L/C Ward, W.N.	Oct. 18th 1916.
A/6276 Pte. Mason, C.	Oct. 12th 1916.

Wounded in Action............64.

Missing..................... 1.

In the Field.
Nov. 2nd 1916.
............W E Slett............Major,
Commanding 16th (S) Bn. Manchester Regiment.

VOLUME XIII.

SECRET.

WAR DIARY.

FOR THE MONTH OF NOVEMBER.

16TH BN. MANCHESTER REGIMENT.

5-12-1916.   R.E. Roberts Captain,
              Commanding 16th (S) Bn Manchester Regiment.

Army Form C. 2118.

WAR DIARY
or
INTELLIGENCE SUMMARY
(Erase heading not required.)

16th (S) Bn. MANCHESTER REGT.

VOLUME XIII - November - Page 1.

Place	Date	Hour	Summary of Events and Information	Remarks and references to Appendices
TRENCHES.	Nov. 1-5		In Left front of BELLACOURT Sector. - Quiet. Distribution of Coys. FRONT:- Left - Centre - Right. C. Coy. B. Coy. D. Coy. Reserve - A. Coy.	
BAILLEULVAL.	6		Relieved by 17th Mcho & marched to Billets in BAILLEULVAL. - Divisional Reserve.	
	7-8		Training.	
	9-11.		Bad weather caused considerable falling in of Trenches, so had to supply working parties.	
TRENCHES	12		Relieved 17th Mcho in left front of BELLACOURT Sectr. Distribution of Coys. FRONT:- Left - Centre - Right. C. Coy. B. Coy. A. Coy. Reserve - D. Coy.	
	13.		Hun discharged on our Right at 3.0 a.m. + on left at 6.0 p.m. - Boche shelled a little in retaliation but not very much.	
	14-14.		Quiet.	
BELLACOURT	15		Relieved by 17th Mcho & went into B'de Reserve at BELLACOURT. Distribution of Coys. A. B. + C. in BELLACOURT. - D. Co. in front strong points.	
	19-23		Supplied working parties daily for the R.E.	
TRENCHES.	24.		Relieved 17th Mcho in left front of BELLACOURT Sector. Left. Centre. Right. D. Co. B. Co. A. Coy. Reserve C. Coy. FRONT :-	

Army Form C. 2118.

16th (S) Bn. Manchester Regt.

WAR DIARY
or
INTELLIGENCE SUMMARY
(Erase heading not required.)

Volume XIII - November - Page 2.

Place	Date	Hour	Summary of Events and Information	Remarks and references to Appendices
Trenches.	Nov. 26-29. 30.		Quiet - Both active with T.M's. Relieved by 18th Mphs. & ordered to Divisional Reserve - H.Q. B.V.C. Coys at Bailleulval, A + D. Coys at Basseux. Casualties during the month. Killed - Officers - O.R. 1 (Pte Aldred J.) 24016 Wounded 1 (2/Lieut T.A.H. Nash slightly - at duty) 5 (1 (Accidental - self-) inflicted.	

R.E. Roberts Capt.
Commdg. 16th (S) Bn Manchester Regt.

VOLUME XLV.

SECRET.

WAR DIARY.

FOR THE MONTH OF DECEMBER

16TH BN. MANCHESTER REGIMENT.

2-1-1917.   ....Lieut. Colonel,
           Commanding 16th (S) Bn. Manchester Regiment.

Army Form C. 2118.

WAR DIARY
or
INTELLIGENCE SUMMARY
(Erase heading not required.)

16th (S.) Bn. MANCHESTER Regt.
VOLUME XIV
December - Page 1.

Instructions regarding War Diaries and Intelligence Summaries are contained in F.S. Regs., Part II. and the Staff Manual respectively. Title Pages will be prepared in manuscript.

Place	Date 1916	Hour	Summary of Events and Information	Remarks and references to Appendices
BAILLEULVAL	Dec 1-5		2 Divisional Reserve - H.Q. B & C. Coy in BAILLEULVAL - A & D. Coys in BASSEUX.	
	6		Relieved 14th M/chrs in Left Front of BELLACOURT Sector.	
	6-12		Distribution of Coys - Front Line & Support - Left - Centre - Right. B.Coy in reserve. D. C. A.	
	12		Relieved by 17th M/chrs - took over B'lt Reserve dispositions in BELLACOURT - the 4 pcts from 14th M/chrs. - B.Coy - the pcts - Boundary - STARFISH - BURNT FARM - Orchard.	
	12-17		Supplied Working Parties for A. C. & D. Coys - H.Q.	
	18		Relieved 15th M/chrs in Left Front of BELLACOURT Sector.	
			Distribution of Coys - Front line & Support. Left Centre - Right. A Coy in Reserve. B. C. D.	
	18-24		Relieved by 17th M/chrs in Reserve at BAILLEULVAL - H.Q. and D. Coy - BASSEUX B & C Coy	
	24		Training	
	24-29		Relieved 15th M/chrs in Left front of BELLACOURT Sector	
	30		Distribution of Coys - Front Line & Support Left - Centre - Right. D. Coy in Reserve. B. - C. - A.	
	30-31			
			CASUALTIES during the month Killed 60716 Pte LAUD, C.R. 24th (B Coy)	
			Wounded 6717 - WILLIAMS, F. 20th (E Coy)	
			16229 - KINGSTON, C. 21st (B Coy).	

WSister, Lt Col
Commdg. 16th (S) Bn M/chester Regt.

SECRET   OPERATION ORDER NO.G.1. BY CAPTAIN R.B.ROBERTS
            COMMANDING 16TH (S) BATT.(1ST) MANCHESTER REGIMENT, DEC 11/16.
            ─────────────────────────────────

1. 16th Manchesters will be relieved by the 18th Manchesters on the 12th
   December.

2. 16th Manchesters will take over billets and posts of BRIGADE RESERVE
   in BELLACOURT from 17th Manchesters.
   DISTRIBUTION OF COMPANIES IN BELLACOURT:-
            A.Company................As before.
            B.   "   ....The 4 Posts.
            C.   "   ....As before.
            D.Coy.   ....In billets occupied by B.Coy before.

   Re.1. Lewis Gunners, Signallers, Scouts & Snipers, and H.Q.Squadrs will be
         relieved first as usual.
         Of the Companies, the RESERVE COMPANY will be relieved by a Company
         of the 18th Manchester first.
         GUIDES: 1 Guide per Lewis Gun Team to be at ends of trenches at
                  8.30 am as follows:-
                          OSIERS Sector........ENGINEER STREET.
                          RAVINE, EPSOM, & CHANCERY LANE........QUARRY STREET.
         Companies move off as battalion boiler to complete to their Company
         Sector. One Officer to report at Bn. H.Q.rs. from each Company when
         Relief is completed.
         Usual precautions to be taken as to Aircraft, March Discipline, etc
         Officers' Trench Kits, and Mess Kits, to be at BRETENCOURT LOADING
         POINT at 9 am.

   Re.2. Gas N.C.Os to proceed to take over Gas Arrangements in BRIGADE
         RESERVE SECTOR when relieved by Gas N.C.Os of 18th Manchesters
         to-night.
         1 N.C.O. per Company and 1 N.C.O. from H.Q.Coy., to be detailed by
         Acting R.S.M., will proceed to BELLACOURT to take over billet and
         trench stores at 7.30 am.

         TRANSPORT. First Wagon leaves BRETENCOURT at 11 am.
                     Q.M. will arrange to have Blankets and Officers' Kits
                     in BELLACOURT.
                     ─────────────

         Orderly Room to-morrow will be held at 3 pm in BELLACOURT.

                                                      ....Capt & Act.Adjt.
                                                          D. G.

Copies to:
         4 Companies.
         M.O.
         Signalling Officer.
         S.S.O.
         Intelligence Officer.
         Bombing Officer.
         Q.M.
         T.O.
         Act.R.S.M.
         O.C.17th Manchesters.
         O.C.18th Manchesters.
         (File Copy).

O.C. 18th Manchester

OPERATION ORDER NO.G.13 BY CAPTAIN R.E.ROBERTS,
COMMANDING 16TH (S) BATTALION, MANCHESTER REGIMENT.

Dec.5th 1916.

1. The 16th Manchesters will relieve the 18th Manchesters on the 6th instant in the Line.

2. DISTRIBUTION OF COMPANIES.

    A.Coy................OSIERS.
    D. " ....RAVINE.
    C. " ....EPSOM.
    B. " ....RESERVE.

3. ORDER OF MARCH.

    Lewis Gunners leave BAILLEULVAL at 7-30 a.m.
    Signallers   -do-   -do-   7-45 a.m.
    Snipers & Bombers   -do-   8- 0 a.m.
    B.Company   -do-   9- 0 a.m.
    C. "   -do-   9-15 a.m.(via QUARRY STREET)
    A. "   leave BASSEUX at   9-40 a.m.(via ENGINEER)
    D. "   -do-   9-55 a.m.(via QUARRY)

4. GAS N.C.O'S.
    1 Gas N.C.O. per Company, and Gas N.C.O. from H.Q.Coy. will report at 18th Manchesters Headquarters at 6 o'clock to-night, to take over Gas Arrangements.

(SHEET NO. 2.)

5. Acting R.S.M. and 1 N.C.O. per Company will leave BAILLEULVAL at 7-1_
(BASSEUX 7-40 am) and proceed to Bn H.Qrs and Coy.Sectors for the
purpose of taking over Trench Stores.

6. BLANKETS.
These will be rolled in bundles of 10, and deposited at Coy.
H.Qrs. at 7-30 am.
Q.M. will arrange transport.
B.Coy's blankets go to BRETENCOURT.

7. TRANSPORT.
First vehicle will leave BAILLEULVAL at 10 am. (This does not
apply to Lewis Gun Handcarts, for which mules will be required.).
Trench Kits and Mess Kit to be collected at 9 am.

.... Capt & Act Adjt,
16th (S) Bn. Manchester Regiment.

SECRET   OPERATION ORDER NO.G.16 BY CAPT. R.E.ROBERTS,
          COMMANDING 16TH (S) BATTALION, MANCHESTER REGIMENT.
                                            Dec.23rd 1916.
....

1. The 16th Manchesters will be relieved by the 18th Manchesters to-morrow, the 24th instant, and will take over billets in BAILLEULVAL and BASSEUX; H.Q., A & D. Coys. in BAILLEULVAL, B. & C. Coys. BASSEUX.
   The 155 O.Rs. (Draft) at present in BAILLEULVAL will remain there until after Christmas.
   C.Q.M.Sgts will proceed to BAILLEULVAL and BASSEUX at 7-30 am to-morrow to take over billets and any billet stores. Particular attention to be paid to "Bombardment Stations".

2. Gas N.C.O's on being relieved by Gas N.C.O's of the 18th Manchesters to-night will proceed to BAILLEULVAL and BASSEUX to take over Gas Arrangements in billets there.

3. Other relief orders will be as usual.
   1 Guide per Lewis Gun position to be at the entrances of trenches, as under, at 8-30 am:-
          OSIERS sector............ENGINEER.
          All others...............QUAREY.
   Careful attention will be paid to march discipline, distance between parties, and taking cover from aircraft, should any be about.

4. Blankets of Reserve Coy. will be rolled in bundles of 10 and be at Loading Point in BRETENCOURT by 8 am.

5. TRANSPORT.
   Mess Cart, and Limber for Officers' Kits, to be at BRETENCOURT by 8 am; also horses for Cookers, and Mules for Lewis Gun Handcarts. Instructions will be issued later as to what riders are required.

6. Officers' Trench Kits and Messes to be at BRETENCOURT loading point by 8-30 am.

                                      ....Capt & Act Adjt
                                      16th (S) Bn. Manchester Regiment.

Copies to:-
   4 Coys.
   M.O.
   Sig. Off.
   L.G.O.
   Int.Off.
   Bombing Off.
   Q.M.
   T.O.
   Act. R.S.M.
   O.C.18th Manchesters.
   (Copy filed)

O.C. 18th Manchester

VOLUME XV.

S E C R E T.

W A R D I A R Y.

F O R T H E M O N T H O F J A N U A R Y.

16TH (S) BATTALION, MANCHESTER REGT.

1-2-17.

.... W Elstob .. Lt. Col.,
Commanding 16th (S) Bn. Manchester Regiment.

WAR DIARY
or
INTELLIGENCE SUMMARY
(Erase heading not required.)

Army Form C. 2118

16TH (S) BN. MANCHESTER REGT VOLUME XVII – Page 1

MARCH – 1917.

Place	Date	Hour	Summary of Events and Information	Remarks and references to Appendices
HALLOY	1917 Mar 1-12		Bn. supplied working parties double tracking railway line from DOULLENS to POMMERA.	
GRENAS	12		Bn. moved to Billets in GRENAS – Bn. Officers Mess formed for first time since arrival in FRANCE.	
	12-18		Supplied some working parties on Mar 1-12.	
MONCHIET	19.		Bn. marched to billets in MONCHIET	
TRENCHES	21		Marched to Trenches in AGNY at 1.30 p.m. + to MERCATEL at 11.15 p.m. where Outpost line was taken over from 19TH K.L.R. Relief being complete at 6.0 a.m. 22nd. Distribution of Coys:– A Coy on Left. D Coy on Right. B Coy in support. C Coy in Reserve.	
	22		Fairly quiet – slow steady shelling by the enemy. Company reliefs at 3.0 a.m. Distribution:– C. Coy on Left – B Co on Right. D Coy in support. A Coy in Reserve.	
	23		Enemy attacked our Right at 4.50 a.m. but were driven off by L.G. + Rifle fire at a cost of 5 O.R. wounded on our side (one of whom, Pte RYAN, has since died) + fate of the enemy known to be wounded. Company reliefs at 2.0 a.m. Distribution:– D. Coy on Left – A. Coy on Right. C. Coy in support. B. Coy in Reserve.	
	24.			
	25.		Slow steady shelling by enemy continued. Company reliefs at 3.0 a.m. Distribution – B. Coy on Left – C. Coy on Right. A. Coy in support. D. Coy in Reserve.	
	26. 27.			

WAR DIARY
or
INTELLIGENCE SUMMARY
(Erase heading not required.)

16th (S) Bn. MANCHESTER RGT.

Army Form C. 2118

MARCH – 1917 – VOLUME XVII – Page 2.

Place	Date	Hour	Summary of Events and Information	Remarks and references to Appendices
TRENCHES	1917 Mar. 28.		Slow steady shelling by enemy continued – 2/Lieut W. CLARK killed in the afternoon, also 35694 Pte OLDFIELD, W.H. In the evening 61515 Pte KEWER, H.T. was killed to kill fire 2nd Bn YORKSHIRE REGT took over the Outpost line, relief being complete 12.30 a.m. – 29.3.17	
BELLACOURT – GROSVILLE	29	3.0 a.m. + 6.0 a.m.	Moved to Billets in BELLACOURT and GROSVILLE which were reached between 3.0 a.m. + 6.0 a.m.	
	30-31		Resting:- Supplied working parties of about 500 for Railway & sundry work.	

CASUALTIES during the month.

OFFICER.
Killed.   2/Lieut W. CLARK – 27.3.17 –

OR

	Killed	
6/35699	Pte W.H. OLDFIELD	27.3.17
B/61739	H.T. KEWER	27.3.17
B/37700	AERYAN (Died of Wounds)	28.3.17

Wounded

D/29476	G. HOFTON	2.3.17
D/40745	J.E PEARSON	23.3.17
D/36393	J. CARTWRIGHT	26.3.17
D/35649	G. REDFORD	26.3.17
B/29111	H. CADMAN	26.3.17
B/33139	J. DINSDALE	26.3.17
9/7228	Sgt. H. KELLY	26.3.17
9/6390	Cpl. G. HULL	29.3.17
C/37002	L/Cpl McMULLIN	27.3.17
C/46725	Pte E. MOORWOOD	27.3.17
D/37103	F HALL (Slightly-at duty)	29.3.17

W.S.J./Stk.
Lt. Col.
Commdg 16th(S) Bn. M/CHSTR. REGT.

VOLUME XVI

S E C R E T.

W A R   D I A R Y.

FOR THE MONTH OF FEBRUARY.

16TH (S) BATTALION, MANCHESTER REGIMENT.

............W E Elstob............Lieut-Colonel
March 2nd 1917.   Commanding 16th (S) Bn. Manchester Regiment.

Army Form C. 2118.

WAR DIARY
or
INTELLIGENCE SUMMARY.
(Erase heading not required.)

16TH (S) Bn. MANCHESTER R.GT.

FEBRUARY - VOLUME XVI - Page 1

Place	Date	Hour	Summary of Events and Information	Remarks and references to Appendices
DAINEVILLE	1917 Feb 1.		Battn. on Working party at DAINEVILLE, grading 60 cm. Railway Line.	
	2.		Marched to WARLUZEL	
	3.		Marched to HALLOY.	
	4-14		Battn. on Working party - double-tracking Railway between DOULLENS & PONNERA	
	15		2 Platoons from each Co. marched to SAULTY.	
			Special training at the Div. School in the new Platoon organization (adopted from the French army)	
			Remainder of Battn. in HALLOY continued work on Railway line.	
	19-24		The 2 Platoons at each Coy. returned from Div. School to HALLOY.	
	25		The whole Battn. continued work on the Railway.	
	26-28		CASUALTIES during the month:-	
			A/40630 L/Cpl. MORTON, S. accidentally wounded by Rifle fire 20-2-17	
			Died of wounds - 21-2-17	
			A/29900 Pte RATHBONE, G. } accidentally wounded by Rifle grenade 23-2-17	
			A/40525 " MITCHELL, G.A. } both remained at duty	

W. Elstob. Lt. Col.
Commdg 16th (S) Bn. Manchester Regt

S E C R E T

WAR DIARY
16th (S) Bn MANCHESTER REGIMENT.

VOLUME XVII
MARCH - 1917.

..........Lieut-Colonel
Commanding 16th (S) Bn Manchester Regiment

Army Form C. 2118.

16th (S) Bn Manchester Regt

WAR DIARY
or
INTELLIGENCE SUMMARY
(Erase heading not required.)

VOLUME XI – Page 1.

Place	Date	Hour	Summary of Events and Information	Remarks and references to Appendices
TRENCHES.	1917 Jan 1st-8th		In left half of BELLACOURT Sector – Relieved on the 4th by the 5th K.O.Y.L.I. & marched to BAVINCOURT Tents.	
	8.		Marched to Billets at WARLUZEL.	
	9-23		Training & reorganisation of Platoons on French model.	
	24.		Battn. (less Transport) moved by 'bus to DAINEVILLE.	
	25-31.		Supplied workingparty for building 60 cm. Railway under the 1st Canadian Pioneer Battn.	
			Casualties during the month. – 40884 Pte Watts. A.V. Wounded slightly (at duty)	

W Elstob Lt. Col.
Comdg 16th (S) Bn Manchester Regt.

VOLUME XVIII

SECRET

WAR DIARY
FOR THE MONTH OF APRIL
16TH (S) BATTALION MANCHESTER REGIMENT

May 1st 1917
..................Lieut-Colonel
Commanding 16th (S) Bn Manchester Regiment.

Army Form C. 2118.

WAR DIARY
or
INTELLIGENCE SUMMARY.
(Erase heading not required.)

17TH (S) BN. MANCHESTER REGT.

VOLUME XVIII. - APRIL - Page 1.

Place	Date	Hour	Summary of Events and Information	Remarks and references to Appendices
GROSVILLE	April 1		Supplied working party of 470 for Railway & other work.	
TRENCHES (HENIN)	2		Marched to HENIN area & relieved the 2nd YORKS. - Relief complete at 4.0 a.m. 3rd.	
	3		Disposition :- D. Coy in Nos 1 & 4 posts, HENIN - A. Coy in No 5 post & immediate support to the Village - B. Coy in support along ARRAS-BAPAUME RD. - C. Coy in reserve in SWITCH LANE.	
	4		Coy Reliefs at 10.0 p.m. Disposition :- B. Coy in Nos 1 & 4 posts. C. Coy in Nos 5 post & immediate support to the Village - A. Coy in support - D. Coy in Reserve.	
	5		Moved posts forward about 500x - Good work by B. Coy.	
	6		Occupied Mill at N.32.4.9 & HENIN - NEUVILLE VITASSE RD. - Good work by C. Coy.	
	7		Handed over posts in & around HENIN to 2nd BEDS. - Relief complete by 3.0 a.m. 8th.	
FICHEUX	8		Marched to Trenches by FICHEUX.	
	9		Commenced Battle by 3rd Army & HINDENBURG LINE.	
MERCATEL	10	1.0 p.m	Received orders to move forward to position S. & MERCATEL & the Eastern side of the road running between MERCATEL & BOISLEUX ST. MARC.	
		1.30 p.m	Received orders to move to position N.W. of HENINEL on the Eastern side of the HINDENBURG LINE. Marched off at 2.0 p.m. & reached Cross Roads W of ST MARTIN SUR COJEUL where M.G. & Lewis gun fire was met with. - Halted & disposed Batt as follows :- B. Coy along NEUVILLE-VITASSE - ST. MARTIN RD. A. B. & C. Coy along NAGPUR TRENCH. - Requested orders & found that the situation was not as anticipated & that we held HINDENBURG LINE from NEPAL TRENCH to the S.E. - Battalion in N.R.	[in]

Army Form C. 2118.

WAR DIARY 16th (S) Bn. MANCHESTER REGT.
or
INTELLIGENCE SUMMARY. VOLUME XVIII – APRIL – Page 2.
(Erase heading not required.)

Place	Date	Hour	Summary of Events and Information	Remarks and references to Appendices
NAGPUR TRENCH	April 10	5.0 p.m	in NAGPUR TRENCH 1/2 the Cross Rds. N.W. of HENIN. Received orders to take up position along NEUVILLE VITASSE – ST MARTIN Rd. – NEUVILLE VITASSE-HENIN Rd. – SIGNIFICATION – C Coy in front saunken road, A & D Coys in 2nd saunken – B Coy in reserve – BEAURAINS – BOIRY BECQUERELLE Rd.	
		10.0 p.m	Received orders to send 1 Coy the remainder up to HINDENBURG LINE to trench down from N.W. of NATAL TRENCH & secure the system known as THE COT on the S.E. side of NATAL TRENCH – A Coy detailed	
	11	4.30 am	A Coy proceeded to HINDENBURG LINE & in conjunction with 1/9th LONDON REGT & 4th MIDDLESEX REGT bombed down to THE COT, securing same at 2.0 p.m.	
		6.30 pm	A Coy relieved by the 1942 Middlesex Regt & rejoined Battn. in NEUVILLE VITASSE-HENIN Rd.	
	12		Handed over to 1st MIDDLESEX REGT & 4th SUFFOLK REGT & marched to billets in BAILLEULVAL	
	13	11.0 am	Marched to billets in SOUASTRE.	
	14		Rest & change up.	
	15			
	16		Training	
	17			
	Fr 18	4.0 am	Received orders to move to NEUVILLE VITASSE area – Arrived from SOUASTRE at 12.0 noon	See Appendix I
	18–24		See Report on Operation, attached.	
	24–25		In HINDENBURG LINE (THE COT) behind HENINEL.	
	25	11.0 am	Arrived at ARRAS Entraining there at 10.30 pm for ST POL.	
	26	9.30 am	Arrived ST POL detrained & marched to billets in CROISETTES.	

Army Form C. 2118

WAR DIARY
or
INTELLIGENCE SUMMARY
(Erase heading not required.)

16TH ① Bn. MANCHESTER Regt.

VOLUME XVIII - APRIL - Page 3

Instructions regarding War Diaries and Intelligence Summaries are contained in F. S. Regs., Part II. and the Staff Manual respectively. Title Pages will be prepared in manuscript.

Place	Date	Hour	Summary of Events and Information	Remarks and references to Appendices
CROISETTE	April 29-30		Resting & cleaning up. CASUALTIES during the month – April 1st to 20th See Appendix II. " 21st to 30th III	See Appendix II. — III

W.L.R.G Lt. Col.
Comndg. 16th ① Bn. MANCHESTER Regt.

SECRET

22/4/17

Operation Orders E 2.
By Lieut- Col. W Elstob. M.C
Commanding. D I G.

[A.]

1. ASSEMBLING POSITION
The Bn will assemble at road running through N23 d, N29 b, a & c tonight at a time to be notified later.

DISPOSITION OF COYS.
A & B Coys on left of Cross Roads at N 29 a 8 5. C & D Coys on the right of those cross roads. A on extreme left. D on extreme right.

Bn H.Q. will be about N 29 b 2 4. Right flank of B Coy and left flank of C Coy to be at least 50 yds from the cross roads.

D Coy to leave a gap at cross roads at N 29 a 0 5 and N 29 c 4 9

2. MOPPING UP PARTIES.
O.C. A Coy will detail the following mopping up parties

To be attached to 2nd R.S.F. 2 Officers and 8 parties of 1 N.C.O. and 6 men each.

To be attached to 17th Manchester Regt. 2 parties of 1 N.C.O. and 6 men each.

These parties will rejoin A Coy on completion of cleaning up work allotted to them by the R.S.F. & 17th Manchester Regt. respectively.

3. SUPPORTS FOR FRONT LINE BNS.
B Coy will maintain touch with O.C. 2nd R.S.F. by connecting files and be ready to reinforce at any moment on instructions from O.C. 2nd R.S.F.
C Coy will maintain touch with O.C. 17th Manchester Regt by connecting files, and be ready to reinforce at any moment on instructions from O.C. 17th Manchester Regt.
In the event of reinforcements being called for by either Bns, O.C. Coy will act upon same and report action to this Bn HQ.
Should both B & C Coys have to proceed forward, information will at once be sent from Bn HQ to O.C. 18th Manchester Regt, who will move forward to consolidate line as in para 4.

4. MOVING FORWARD & CONSOLIDATION.
Coys will move forward in Artillery Formation and consolidate positions in support at times as stated.

A. Coy (less mopping up parties) plus 2 platoons of B Coy move at Zero + 15 and consolidate Quarry (inclusive) to Divisional Boundary at O 25 a 2.8.

B Coy. (less 2 platoons) will move at Zero + 25 and consolidate from N 30 b 5 2 (junction with A Coy) to N 30 d 5 7 using old German Trench if suitable.

C Coy will move at Zero + 35 and consolidate from N 30 d 5 7 to N 36 b 0 8 having one platoon to south of road at latter point.

D Coy will move at Zero + 45 and consolidate line from N 30 c 6.5 to N 30 c 7 2.

5. Bn HQ will move at Zero + 55 to position about N 30 c 7 2.

6. **MACHINE GUNS.**
1½ Sections of Machine Guns Coy. will go forward with A Coy & select suitable sites in or near the Quarry.
½ Section will move forward with D Coy. and select suitable sites in D Coys. position or C Coys. position.

7. <u>R.E's</u>
One section will proceed to A Coy in the Quarry when sent for by R.E. Officer, who will accompany O.C. A. Coy
One section will proceed to C. Coy when sent for by R.E. Officer who will accompany O.C. C. Coy

8. <u>DRESS</u>
Fighting Order. Packs with Great-Coats will be dumped near the Tank at N27 b 1 9
Each Man will carry spade or pick; in proportion 4 spades to 1 pick.
2 Bombs etc, as previously ordered.

9. <u>REPORTS AND COMMUNICATIONS</u>
Coys in the front line of the Bde will send reports every ½ hour to O.C. Bn they may be attached to. Copies of messages sent to be retained.
Any information obtained in whatever position the Coy may be, to be forwarded to nearest Bn H.Q. as frequently as possible.
In all cases Reports should say whether touch has been

made with flanking Bdes & Bns. CONTACT AEROPLANES may be recognized by having one black band under the right lower plane.

10. MEDICAL COLLECTING STATION is at N 22 d 7.8. Walking wounded collecting station is in Mercatel at M 29 d 9. <u>Stretcher bearers</u>. 2 Stretcher Bearers and 1 Stretcher will move with each Coy; remainder with H.Q. Coy.

11. <u>PRISONERS</u>. Advanced Divisional Collecting Station will be at M 24 d 8 7 (NEAR NEUVILLE MILL). Front line Bns will escort them to Support Bn, but under no circumstances will their escorts go further back than the Support Bn.
Support Bn (DIG) will send escorts with prisoners back to Divisional Cage via Bde H.Q. at N 22 d 5.4. Returning to their Coys from Divisional Cage. Parties of Prisoners should be collected into groups of about 20, and an escort of 2 men sent with each group.

12. TIME Each Coy will send a Representative with 2 Watches to Bn H.Q. immediately on receiving orders to move from present area. (N 27 b) to synchronise Watches.

13. REFERENCE MAP 51. B. SW.

R. Gibbon
Cpt. 2/4
A/g

Copies to
A. B. C + D. Coys
QM.
a/R.S.M.
Bde
2nd R.S.F.
17th M/CHR. Regt.
18th M/CHR. Regt.

APPENDIX I to
REPORT on OPERATIONS of
16TH (S) BN MANCHESTER RGT.
12 noon April 18th to
12 noon — 24th

[B]

Reconnaissance of Left position.

April 23. 6.30am After Bn H.Q. had halted at N.29.d.8.9 I went along to the left of our old front line & down the trench going E from about (N.30.a.9.6) Some 150x down that trench I found another trench leading off to the left & a few yards along that trench I found Lt WRIGHT of the 2nd R.S.F. with their Bn H.Q. Coy. — He informed me that Col McCONAGHY & the Adjt had gone forward & had not been seen since though he had heard that both of them were wounded.
A number of men of R.S.F. 16th & 14th Mch. R. scattered about in isolated parties in shell holes — Enemy very active with snipers & M.G's which

[This map reference should read N.30.a.9.2]

[C]

it appeared had held attack up.

B'de signals got a line up to this point (N.20.a.91 approx) & I communicated with B'de Major mentioning that situation was very obscure but that I was endeavouring to clear it up & that a flank attack up the valley from the right would probably clear the enemy out —

Received instructions to take charge & organise that attack.

Instructed Lt WRIGHT to take charge of 2nd R.S.F. & any other parties of men near him & to organise a defensive position along the trench he was in, also to thin out the men & form them into groups under a N.C.O. or a senior private.

Then went forward to try discover where our pack [?] line actually had got to — on the way met Capt HENDRIE of Stokes Mortar battery & explained my intention of organising an attack up the valley, arranging for him to bring pack to bear

[Over]

on the left to occupy the attention of the enemy as soon as he saw party approaching up the valley. Capt HENDRIE then went to reconnoitre positions for his guns.

I then went on towards the QUARRY &, leaving the trench, found up some more isolated parties of men in shell holes — It was necessary to crawl the whole time as ground was covered with M.G. & Rifle fire — I could not find any officers so instructed each party that I came across to continue crawling along the shell holes that they were in & to hold on to them.

In the most forward shell hole that I reached I found one of our Sgts & 3 men. This Sgt informed me that the enemy were only about 25 yds away. He pointed out where he thought our left flank was (about N30 d14) & told me that at about 8.0 a.m. 60 Boche had attacked from a trench but had been driven off by Lewis Gun & Rifle fire —

He said it was impossible to move from the shell holes without being shot.

I asked the Sgt whether he thought he was strong enough to hold the Boche on his immediate front & he replied "Certainly sir, we've done it once & we can do it again."

I told him that I was going to organise a flank attack up the valley from the copse on the right & that he was to be ready to give covering fire with the men around him — He thoroughly understood the position & the tactics to be employed.

At this time (about 9.0 a.m.) enemy apparently did not know where his own line was as he was shelling positions held by his troops.

I then returned to my Bn. H.Q. at N.29.d.7.9. & carried on as per report already sent.

"REPORT ON OPERATIONS [25-4-17] **Appendix I.**
of 16TH Bn. MANCHESTER RGT.
from 12 noon Wed 18th April to
12 noon Tues 24th April.

April 18th — 12 noon   Marched from SOUASTRE to Trenches near NEUVILLE VITASSE, arriving there at 2·0 a.m. 19th.

19th   2 p.m.   Moved to Trenches in THE COT (N.24L).

20-22   Remained in THE COT

22   10·0 pm   Coys started moving to Assembly position on SUNKEN RD E of HENINEL extending from N.29.c.15 to N.23.d.83. In position by 3·0 a.m. 23rd

23   4·45 a.m.   Attack commenced by 90th Bde. on German position E. of HENINEL

SEE O.O.   over a frontage of 1500ˣ, from
No. E.2   N.24.d.20 to N.35.b.1.6, the objectives
ATTACHED.   about 1500ˣ distant —
(LETTERED   Bde Dispositions being 19th Mchstr Rgt
"A".)   on Right — 2nd R.S.F. on Left —
16th Mchstr Rgt in immediate support & to consolidate line of Strong points from QUARRY in N.30.b to SUNKEN RD at N.36.b.18. Also to supply 8 Mopping up parties to 2nd R S F + 2 Mopping up parties to 19th Mchstr Rgt —
18th Mchstr Rgt also in Support.
16th Mchstr Rgt dispositions were C Coy on Right, B. Coy in [Centre]

centre, A. Coy on Left – D. Coy in support

5.0 am	A Coy moved from ASSEMBLY position to flanks of R.E.	
5.10 am	B	
5.20 am	C	14th M/clot Regt
5.30 am	D	C Coy
5.40 am	Bn H Q	D

Immediately on leaving ASSEMBLY position a number of casualties were caused by M.G. fire.

6.22 am Received message from Adjutant of 14th M/chine Regt. asking for 2 platoons to be sent forward to reinforce –

O.C. D. Coy instructed to send 2 platoons up in accordance with 90th Bde O.O. 64.

6.30 am Bn H Q reached our old front line (Cable Trench) & halted at N29d84 to get information as to the situation which was obscure.

10.0 am After personal reconnaissance by the C.O., from which it appeared

SEE REPORT ON RECONNAISSANCE (LETTERED "B") that the left of the line was held from about N.30 a 81 through N.30 b 3.4 & back in direction of WANCOURT TOWER, a flanking attack was decided upon from the right up the Valley through N.36 a 10 PICTURE GROUND in N.30 c & d. & towards the QUARRY in N.30 b. —

[Orders]

10.15am Orders issued to O.C. D Coy, DRAT, attached to us, to carry out this flank attack, & arrangements made for covering Lewis Gun & Rifle fire from detachment of our men in shell holes about N.30 a 9.2

11.15am Counter attack developed by enemy on the left & appeared to be gaining ground by WANCOURT TOWER –
Sniping & M.G. fire on our right increased

11.25am Orders sent to O.C. D Coy, DRAT to cancel his flank attack & to hold himself in readiness to counter-attack WANCOURT TOWER should it fall.
At the same time O.C. C Coy, DRAT ordered to send two platoons to trench running E from our position at about N.30 a 9.6 to form a defensive flank.
Orders sent to M.G.O. DIRT, attached to us, to send 1 gun along to that position for same purpose.

3.0pm Received orders from 90th Bde to assemble Bn. in Trench dug by 17th Middx gdn night of 21/22 at about N.29 d 20 & N.29 d 25, & re-organise

4.30pm Received Verbal orders from Bde Major to take part in new attack at 6.0 p.m. (& consolidate)

[4]

& consolidate some position allotted to us in the morning's attack.

5.15 pm Major CAMPBELL of 18th K.L.R. informed us that he had received instructions to carry out work of consolidation which we had been detailed to do.

5.45 pm Telephoned B'de to the effect that we had only 3 Coy. Officers & 60 men then available besides Bn. H.Q. with exception of 2 platoons lent to DUST in the morning & which had not returned at that time

5.55 pm Received Telephone message from B'de to return to Trenches in "THE COT."

6.0 pm Men started moving to THE COT in small parties

6.45 pm Bn H.Q. moved to THE COT arriving at 7.45 p.m.

8.30 pm On orders from G.O.C. 90th B'de guides were provided to conduct 89th B'de to positions around HENINEL.

April 24th.

12 noon. Some of our men from positions in shell holes in advance of our old front line reported back in small parties during the morning.
[Information]

Information gathered from these men shows that they were holding positions in shell holes about N.30.d.45 & N.30.b.41.

The party in N.30.d.45 had 2 Lewis Guns which they used with good effect firing down the SUNKEN RD. running through N.30.b & O.25.a. This party also reports that they were practically surrounded by the enemy & were under our own & the enemy's barrage at different times. These parties appear to have been the furthest forward of our troops.

W. Elstob Lt Col
Commdg 16th Bn MANCHESTER Regt

16th (S) Bn Manchester Regiment.

CASUALTY LIST

```
C/46652  Pte Levey I.      Killed in Action.  5.4.17.
A/41822  L/Cpl Clarke A.R. Killed in Action  11.4.17.


A/36992  Pte Haslam J.     Wounded in Action.  3.4.17
C/39928  Pte Mousley J.A.  Wounded in Action.  6.4.17
C/28384  Pte Holmes W.        -do-              5.4.17.
C/24713  Pte Wilson C.E.      -do-              6.4.17
A/79     Pte McNally J.       -do-              7.4.17.
A/3933   Pte Taylor A.        -do-              7.4.17
C/35223  Pte Glover P.        -do-              6.4.17
C/45020  Pte Tatham C.E.      -do-              6.4.17
A/26656  Pte Mather W.        -do-             12.4.17
A/27050  Pte Disley H.        -do-             11.4.17
B/36640  Pte Green            -do-             11.4.17.


D/7345   Pte Elsworth H. Wounded slightly at Duty. 4.4.17
A/6256   Cpl Hodge J.         -do-              5.4.17
C/38696  Pte Nuttall H.       -do-              5.4.17
B/41839  Pte Merriman A.P.    -do-              7.4.17.
```

APPENDIX II.

CASUALTY LIST (Continued).

The undermentioned Men Reported Missing believed Wounded 23.4.17.

A/27165 Pte Gray A.
B/6676 Cpl Sheard G.
C/43115 Pte Bibbs R.
C/39921 Pte Shaw J.
C/43092 Pte Widdowes A.
C/41850 Pte Brunt A. E.
C/6787 L/Cpl Norbury
C/723 Pte Stevens C.

B/35658 L/Cpl McDougall F.
B/41834 Pte Heath A.G.
C/40905 Pte Drew A.
C/6655 L/Cpl Mills W.
C/41861 Pte Gibbons R.H.
A/40898 Pte Bush T.C.

The undermentioned N.C.O's and men reported Wounded slightly at Duty.

C/6386 Sgt Horford T.
B/33385 Pte Gartside R.

A/43029 Pte Kindleysides H.J.
B/40831 Pte Musson G.

APPENDIX III

16th (S) Bn Manchester Regiment.

CASUALTY LIST

F. Rylands.   "Wounded in Action" 21.4.17
(Died of Wounds 25.4.17)

Captain R.H.Megson	"Killed in Action"	23.4.17
Captain L.F.Wilson	do	23.4.17
Lieutenant C.W.K.Hook	do	23.4.17
2/Lieutenant J.A.Ingram	do	23.4.17
Captain W.T.D.Wickham	"Wounded in Action"	23.4.17
2/Lieutenant J.L.L.Smith	do	do
" W Laughland	do	do
" R.A.M.J. de C.MacDonnell.	do	do
" J.A.Smith	do	do
" H.R.W. Smith	do	do
" G.M. Harvey	do	do
" F.E.Caiger		

C/27470	Cpl	Sandiford T.	"Killed in Action"	21.4.17
C/39972	Pte	Low C.	do	do
C/19244	"	Royle A.	do	do
A/27349	"	Ogden H.	do	22.4.17
A/26484	L/Cpl	Peterson S.	do	do
A/7384	Pte	Murdock A.	do	do
A/29900	"	Rathbone G.	do	23.4.17
A/6232	L/Sgt	Dawson H.	do	do
A/6403	Pte	Mayors J.	do	do
A/27128	L/Cpl	Gibson H.	do	do
~~A/27100~~	~~Pte~~	~~Collinge E.~~	do	do
A/43025	Pte	Harrison H	do	do
A/33270	"	Bell F.W.	do	do
B/32984	"	Dobson F	do	do
B/37980	"	Moores J.	do	do
B/7355	Cpl	Bell W.	do	do
C/43080	Sgt	Hardman J.E.	do	do
C/19321	L/Cpl	Barrow J.	do	do
C/538	L/Cpl	Caley C.	do	do
C/27045	Pte	Holliday A.	do	do
C/34101	"	Power L.	do	do
C/23185	"	Smalley J.	do	do
C/6743	"	Fosbrocke J.	do	do
C/35554	"	Schofield W.E.	do	do
C/1247	"	Spencer W.	do	do
C/47489	"	Hickey E.	do	do
D/43065	"	Gent H.	do	do
D/29457	"	Collins J.	do	do
C/25273	"	Collins W.	do	do
D/34709	"	Lancaster J.	do	do
D/18207	"	Sandham T.	do	do
C/2850	L/Cpl	Thompson G.H.	"Wounded in Action"	23.4.17
C/32610	Pte	Jackson A.V.	do	22.4.17
D/29484	"	Wilkins W	do	do
A/7068	A/C.S.M.	Willis A.	do	23.4.17
A/6603	Sgt	Eavis W.	do	do
A/1667	Cpl	Quinliven J.	do	do
A/34922	Pte	Williams G.	do	do
A/41852	"	Hicks J.	do	do
A/17652	"	Hockaday F.L.	do	do
A/10404	"	Harding R.D.	do	do
A/40907	"	Flint M.	do	do
A/40849	"	Parkin J.	do	do
A/46819	"	Hunt H.	do	do
A/34879	"	Lister E.	do	do
A/33502	"	Stone R.	do	do
A/36832	"	Stone U.	do	do
A/7693	"	Goss T.J.	do	do
A/1248	L/Sgt	Pearce A	do	do
A/41819	L/Cpl	Watts T.		

CASUALTY LIST (continued)

The undermentioned N.C.O's and men Wounded in Action 23.4.17.

A/29463 Pte Hough W.
A/6250   "   Gresty A.
A/17226 L/C Stansby T.A.
A/40847 Pte Parkin J.
A/47279 "   Kershaw C
B/46871 "   Wellbourne J.H.
B/43016 Cpl Patient A.
B/16922 L/C Clarke F.W.
B/43002 Pte Aldous A.
B/1852   "   Barnes F.
B/18472 "   Ferns J.E.
B/16421 Cpl Godwin H.
B/8042 Pte Ashworth A.
B/36581 "   Perry T.E.
B/27307 "   Green O.
A/33680 Pte Coutts J.
C/6769 Sgt Lawrenson F.
C/6808 L/Cpl Stonehewer R.
D/6989 L/Cpl Gosling A.
D/40859 Pte Stafford G.W.
D/41876 Pte Luckham E.H.
D/43059 L/Cpl Paden J.
D/37809 Pte Parkin F.W.
D/43067 Pte Turner E.
D/6991 Pte Griffiths A.   24.3.17.
C/34018 Pte Potts F.F.
C/29622 Pte Travis C.
C/27486 Pte Hamer T.
C/39948 L/Cpl Grimshaw H.
C/43047 Pte Grisdale G.
C/35715 Pte Choularton J.
C/43087 Pte Robinson H.F.
C/35207 Pte Calderbank A.
C/41854 Pte Blachford N.C. 26.4.17

A/27232 Pte Lilley J.
A/41818 L/Cpl Bates W.H.
A/25177 Pte Edge F.
A/43030   "   Little A.
B/6647 L/Cpl Maddocks
B/43010 Cpl Quinn M.
B/43102 L/Cpl Barsby J.
B/40913 Pte Gratton F.W.
B/41841 Pte Oldfield B.S.
B/33222   "   Colley H.
B/41840   "   Nesbitt J.
B/40817 L/Cpl Lupton W.
B/29061 Pte Simpson J.
B/35488 Pte Campbell S.
B/37929 L/Sgt Watson G.
C/6325 Sgt Williams S.R.
C/19704 Cpl Billington H.
C/43075 Pte Griffin A.
D/7064 L/Cpl Tysoe G.
D/8077 L/Cpl Burtenshaw R.
D/43112 L/Cpl Sermon A
D/18147 Pte Hewitt H.
D/43062 Pte Dickinson J.
A/33488 Pte Bell R.E.
C/346 L/Cpl Burns J.A.
C/11291 Pte Taylor W.H.
A/35171 Pte Goodman J.
C/35717 Pte Porter J.
B/30249 Pte Casey P.
C/2789 Cpl Brown F.
C/6855 L/Cpl Crompton S
C/46817 Pte Hopkinson A.H.
B/33265 Pte Wright H.
A/27100 - Collinge E

The undermentioned N.C.O's and Men "Reported Missing in Action. 23.4.17.

A/1473 Cpl Bowden W.
A/25396 Pte Shore W.
A/41856 Pte Gunn A.E.
A/40867 Pte Storey F.
A/40877 Pte Townsend E.
A/7665 Pte Nuttall J.
A/41824 L/Cpl Flower A.E.
A/25227 Pte Hindley G.
A/7436 Pte Boardman E.
A/33713 L/Cpl Dobson W.
A/26101 Pte Pickford W.
A/41823 Pte Emerton A.O.
A/43032 Pte Potts J.
B/27421 Pte Dunkerley E.
C/27114 Pte Wyatt W.
C/39777 Pte Wrigley F.
C/29141 Pte Dover J.B.
~~C/27281 Pte Craig J.W.~~
C/43113 Pte Smith F.

A/6227 L/Cpl Clegg G.R.
A/38738 Pte Whitehead J.
A/32554 Pte Davies H.
A/6410 Pte Murray J.
~~A/35171 Pte Goodman J.~~
A/41821 Pte Bush E.N.
A/27270 L/Cpl Slater H.
A/40828 Pte Mitchell G.A.
A/41828 Pte Gardiner A.E.
A/23082 Pte Estell T.H.
A/25134 Pte Young F.
A/43100 Pte Dawson H.
B/20272 Pte Birtles T.
C/35587 Pte Ridgway A.
C/38634 Sgt Gaynon E.
C/41851 Pte Caunt A.
D/47172 Pte Newbold H.
B/34969 Pte Crompton R.

The undermentioned N.C.O's and Men Reported Missing believed Killed in Action 23.4.17.

A/7074 Sgt Ashton C.E.
C/7556 L/Cpl Worsley S.
C/39993 Pte Platt J.
C/8460 Pte Buckley H.

C/7424 Sgt Bailey P.J.
C/43081 Pte Lodge A.M.
C/18737 Pte Thompson A.
C/27185 Pte Edwards J.

VOLUME XIX

SECRET

WAR DIARY
FOR THE MONTH OF MAY.
16th (S) BATTALION, MANCHESTER REGIMENT.

June 1, 1917.   ....Major
                    Commanding 16th (S) Bn. Manchester Regiment.

Army Form C. 2118.

WAR DIARY

16th (9) Bn. MANCHESTER REGT.

MAY - 1917.

INTELLIGENCE SUMMARY

VOLUME XIX — Page 1.

(Erase heading not required.)

Instructions regarding War Diaries and Intelligence Summaries are contained in F.S. Regs., Part II. and the Staff Manual respectively. Title Pages will be prepared in manuscript.

Place	Date 1917	Hour	Summary of Events and Information	Remarks and references to Appendices
	MAY.			
CROISETTES.	1 - 2		Bn. less D. Coy in billets at CROISETTES — Training.	
			D. Coy — at BACHIMONT — Wood - cutting.	
QUOEUX	3.		Bn. less D. Coy marched to billets in QUOEUX & HAUT. MAISNIL — arrived 3.30 p.m.	
	4.		D. Coy rejoined Bn. from BACHIMONT.	
	4 - 19		Training.	
CROISETTES	20		Marched to CROISETTES — arrived 1.30 p.m. (A.D. Coy billeted in EPS).	
HESTRUS	21		Marched to HESTRUS — arrived 1.30 p.m.	
WESTREHEM	22		Marched to WESTREHEM — arrived 12.30 p.m.	
	23.		Resting.	
GUARBECQUE	24		Marched to GUARBECQUE — arrived 2.55 p.m.	
LA KREULE	25		Marched to LA KREULE, 2 miles N. of HAZEBROUCK — arrived 2.30 p.m.	
	26 - 30		Training.	
ACQUIN.	31		Moved to billets in ACQUIN — Entrained at CAESTRE — arrived 5.30 p.m.	
			ST. OMER — Buses from there to ACQUIN.	
			AWARDS:- Full List of Honours & awards since arrival of Bn. in France/attached See Appendix I	

R. S. Robert
MAJOR
Comndg. 16th (9) Bn. MANCHESTER REGT.

War Diary - Appendix I

16th (S) Bn. Manchester Regiment.

HONOURS and AWARDS

Officers.

Lieut-Colonel W. Elstob.	M.C.	MONTAUBAN and TRONES WOOD. London Gazette 29.12.16 (3rd Supp: 1.1.17).
Lieut-Colonel C.L.R. Petrie D.S.O.		Mentioned in Dispatches. MONTAUBAN. London Gazette 2.1.17 2nd Supp: 4.1.17.
Capt. E. G. Sotham.	M.C.	MONTAUBAN and TRONES WOOD. London Gazette 29.12.16 (3rd Supp. 1.1.17)
" " "		Mentioned in Dispatches. GENERAL → MARICOURT. Lon: Gaz: 13.6.16. 2nd Supp: 15.6.16.
Capt. G.F.P. Heathcote.		French Croix de Guerre. MONTAUBAN. 11th Corps R.O. 479. 26.8.16.
Capt R.H. Megson.		Mentioned in Dispatches. MONTAUBAN - TRONES WOOD - GUILLEMONT. Lon: Gaz: 2.1.17. 2nd Supp 4.1.17.
" "		Mentioned in Dispatches. FLERS. Supp: to Lon: Gaz: 25.5.17.
Lieut. T.A.H. Nash.		Mentioned in Dispatches. MONTAUBAN. Lon:Gaz: 2.1.17. 2nd Supp: 4.1.17.
2/Lieut S. Kershaw.		Mentioned in Dispatches. FLERS. Supp: to Lon: Gaz 25. 5. 17.
Lieut & Q.M. J.T. Ball.		Mentioned in Dispatches. FLERS. -ditto-.

W.O.s. N.C.O's & Men.

C/6723 C.S.M. Brown F.J.	M.C.	HENINEL - CHERISY. 30th Div. R.O. 2699. 19.5.17.
D/7191 Sgt Pennington T.	D.C.M.	MONTAUBAN - TRONES WOOD. Lon:Gaz:13.2.17 Supp: same date.
D/7111 Sgt Gowan H.	D.C.M.	MONTAUBAN. Lon:Gaz:13.2.17. Supp: same date
D/40861 Pte Snowden F.	D.C.M.	DUBLIN. Lon:Gaz: 23.1.17. 3rd Supp. 24.1.17
B/43008 Sgt Leech R.	D.C.M.	HENIN. 30th Div. R.O. 2643. 27. 4. 17.
A/6424 L/Cpl Riddick W.	M.M.	MARICOURT (Y.3). Lon:Gaz:2.6.16. Supp: 3.6.16.
C/7038 L/Cpl Palmer H.	M.M.	MONTAUBAN 12th Corps R.O.320.17.7.16.
C/6828 Pte Baines G.	M.M.	MONTAUBAN " "
D/7128 Pte Kirkpatrick H.	M.M.	MARICOURT (Y.3) Lon: Gaz:10.10.16. Supp: 11.10.16
A/6683 Sgt Smith R.	M.M.	MARICOURT (Y.3) " " "
B/6636 L/Cpl Jowle R.	M.M.	MONTAUBAN. Lon:Gaz:19.9.16. 3rd Supp:
" " "		Russian Medal St George. 4th Class. GUILLEMONT. 11th Corps R.O. 553. 15.9 16.

HONOURS and AWARDS.   (Sheet 2)

B/7113 Pte Greaves W.	M.M. MONTAUBAN.	Lon:Gaz:14.11.16. 5th Supp. 16.11.16.
C/7599 L/Cpl Bowie D.	M.M. MONTAUBAN.	" " " "
A/6246 L/Cpl Frood C.T.	M.M. MONTAUBAN.	" " " "
A/6368 L/Cpl Dawson S.P.	M.M. MONTAUBAN & TRONES WOOD.	" " " "
B/6676 Cpl Sheard G.	M.M. MONTAUBAN	" " " "
A/6445 Pte Wayne F.	M.M. MONTAUBAN	" " " "
C/6822 Pte Wordsworth G.	M.M. MONTAUBAN	" " " "
D/6712 R.Q.M.S.Allen H.	M.M. TRONES WOOD.	Lon:Gaz:6.2.17. 6th Supp: 19.2.17.
D/6980 Sgt Drabble A.	M.M. BELLACOURT SECTOR.	" " "
A/6235 L/Cpl Deaville A.	M.M. GUILLEMONT.	" " "
B/6527 L/Cpl Mein W.	M.M. MONTAUBAN.	Lon: Gaz: 6.2.17. 6th Supp: 19.2.17. K.in A. sub: to the date of the Award to him by the C in C in the Field.
C/6570 Pte Harding J.T.	M.M. MONTAUBAN.	-ditto-.
B/7374 Sgt Gleave W.	M.M.)	
B/6545 Cpl Proffitt A.	M.M.)	
C/6386 Sgt Horford T.	M.M.) HENINEL - CHERISY.	30th Div. R.O. 2684 12.5.17.
C/29626 Pte Petticrew E.	M.M.)	
C/43073 Pte Flanagan M.	M.M.)	
C/32789 Cpl Brown F.	M.M.)	
C/6735 L/Cpl Dickenson S.	M.M.)	
A/6241 L/Cpl Edge H.	French Medaille Militaire. MONTAUBAN.	30th Div. R.O. 2415. 10.2.17.
A/7025 Sgt Lucas H.J.	Mentioned in Dispatches. FLERS.	Lon:Gaz.Supp 25.5.17.
D/7064 L/Cpl Tysoe G.	Mentioned in Dispatches. FLERS.	" "
C/43051 Pte Scoppie J.D.	Mentioned in Dispatches. FLERS.	" "

VOLUME XX

SECRET
....

W A R   D I A R Y
FOR THE MONTH OF JUNE
16TH (S) BATTALION, MANCHESTER REGIMENT

July 1 1917
..............Wilstob..............Lieut-Colonel
Commanding 16th (S) Bn Manchester Regiment.

Army Form C. 2118.

16TH (1) BN. MANCHESTER REGT.

WAR DIARY
or
INTELLIGENCE SUMMARY

VOLUME XV. JUNE 1917. - Page 1.

(Erase heading not required.)

Instructions regarding War Diaries and Intelligence Summaries are contained in F. S. Regs., Part II. and the Staff Manual respectively. Title pages will be prepared in manuscript.

Place	Date	Hour	Summary of Events and Information	Remarks and references to Appendices
ACQUIN.	1917 June 1-5		Training	
HELLEHOEK	6	9 a.m.	Entrained at ACQUIN at 9 a.m. Detrained at ABEELE-POPERINGHE RD at 2.30 p.m. - marched to billets near HELLEHOEK, W of POPERINGHE - arrived at 6.0 p.m.	
	7-8		Training.	
TORONTO CAMP	9		Marched to TORONTO CAMP - Left at 6.0 p.m. arrived 9.30 p.m.	
	10-13		Provided working parties each night.	
TRENCHES	14.		Relieved 2nd Bn. YORKS. REGN. HOOGE SECTR - Relief complete 4.0 a.m. 15th.	
	15.		Dispositions: A Coy on Rgt, B. Coy in centre, D. Coy on Left. C Coy in Support in Tunnel, Bn. H.Q. at DORMY HOUSE.	
	16-20		Enemy artillery & aircraft active all the time. Enemy infantry quiet.	
OTTAWA CAMP.	21		Relieved by 19th Bn. MCHSTR. REGT. & marched to OTTAWA CAMP. Relief complete 3.30 a.m. 22nd.	
	22		Marched to RENINGHELST STATION - entrained at 9.30 a.m. for WATTEN - Detrained there at 3.0 p.m. & marched to billets in LA PANNE - arrived 5.30 p.m.	
LA PANNE	23-24		Training.	
OTTAWA CAMP	25		Marched to WATTEN & entrained there at 10.0 a.m. for ABEELE. Detrained at ABEELE at 3.0 p.m. & marched to OTTAWA CAMP which was reached at 6.0 p.m.	

Army Form C. 2118.

WAR DIARY
or
INTELLIGENCE SUMMARY

16th (S) Bn Manchester Regt.

Volume XX. June 1917. Page 2.

(Erase heading not required.)

Place	Date	Hour	Summary of Events and Information	Remarks and references to Appendices
LRVE AMP.	June 29.		Marched to CANAL RESERVE CAMP, arrived 10.0 a.m.	
			C & D Coys provided working party to rendezvous at BEDFORD HOUSE at 10.0 p.m. for digging Cable Trench.	See Appendix I.
	30.		A & B Coys provided working party to rendez-vous at ZILLEBEKE BUND at 10.0 p.m. for digging Cable Trench.	See Appendix II.
			HONOURS & AWARDS during the month	
			CASUALTIES during the month	
			Killed. Wounded. Missing.	
			Officers - - -	
			O.R. 9. 40 3	
			(includes 2 slightly, (Believed killed) at duty)	
			W2/E/6 Lt. Col. Commdg. 16th (S) Bn Manchester Regt.	

WAR DIARY - APPENDIX I

16th (S) Bn Manchester Regiment.

HONOURS and AWARDS.

B/17324 L/Cpl COXON H.   MEDAILLE MILITAIRE.   HENINEL - CHERISY
                         II Corps R.O. 568. 2.6.17.

WAR DIARY - APPENDIX II

16th (S) Bn Manchester Regiment.

CASUALTIES. JUNE 1917

A/302888	Pte	Collier M.	K. in A.	15.6.17.
A/302982	Pte	Gale S.C.	"	"
A/10260	Pte	Priestner W.H.	"	16.6.17.
A/302909	Pte	Crompton F.	"	"
B/34850	Pte	Garner J.	"	"
B/32959	L/Cpl	Whitworth E.	"	"
B/48649	Pte	Garrett A.	"	18.6.17
B/35503	L/Cpl	Parkes H.	"	20.6.17.
B/32608	Pte	Taylor O.	"	
A/21444	L/Cpl	Jubb. T.H.	Wounded in Action.	15.6.17.
A/34012	L/Cpl	Davison E.	"	"
A/35039	Pte	Minshull J.	"	"
A/302537	"	Brown C.	"	"
A/302964	"	Galloway J.	"	"
A/25214	"	Hickson W.J.	"	"
A/34002	"	Hollywood A.E.	"	"
A/302989	"	Ring E.	"	"
A/37814	"	Lamb C.	"	"
A/40883	"	White E.	"	"
C/21946	Pte	Nugent L.	"	16.6.17.
A/302903	"	Kilgour R.	"	"
B/29594	"	Knight C.	"	"
B/48745	"	Ambery A.G	"	"
B/35485	"	Benson T.W.	"	"
B/41847	"	Boon H.	"	"
B/20947	"	Ormerod J.T.	"	"
B/34401	"	Rollston W.	"	"
B/40887	"	Whittington	"	"
C/277533	"	Kimberly J.	"	"
B/5539	"	Greenhough J.	"	"
B/29778	"	Wainwright A.E.	"	"
B/43094	Cpl	Stalker J.	"	"
A/43006	Cpl	Fairclough G.	"	17.6.17.
A/6256	L/Sgt	Hodge H.	"	18.6.17.
B/6677	Pte	Sinclair I.E.	"	"
B/37755	"	Whittaker W.	"	"
C/32623	"	Seddon E.	"	"(slightly at duty
B/43067	"	Turner E.	"	19.6.17
B/40876	"	Thorniwell B.	"	21.6.17
D/45322	"	Hyde J.	"	"
D/40863	"	Smith G.W.	"	22.6.17.
D/20520	Cpl	Partington F.B.	"	"
D/41880	L/Cpl	Nice F.G.	"	"
D/33682	Pte	Evans R.	"	"
D/34214	"	Kirk W.	"	"
D/43095	"	Snaith A.	"	"
D/29672	"	Broadbent J.	"	"
D/40855	"	Radley W.	"	"(slightly at duty
D/7292	L/Cpl	Bostwick W.	"	
A/27232	Pte	Lilley J.	Missing in A.	15.6.17
A/303011	"	Hancock J.C.	"	"
A/23199	"	Ward H.	"	"

These 3 missing men are believed killed as they were last seen in DAVIDSON TRENCH on the night of 14th/15th June when Enemy were shelling that area and several other Casualties occurred at the time. On search being made the remains of 3 bodies were discovered but no identification was obtainable.

VOLUME XXI

SECRET

WAR DIARY
FOR THE MONTH OF JULY
16TH (S) BATTALION, MANCHESTER REGIMENT

August 5th 1917.

..................Lieut-Colonel
Commanding 16th (S) Bn Manchester Regiment.

WAR DIARY

16TH (①) Bn MANCHESTER Regt.

Army Form C. 2118

INTELLIGENCE SUMMARY

VOLUME XXI – July – Page 1.

(Erase heading not required.)

Place	Date	Hour	Summary of Events and Information	Remarks and references to Appendices
CANAL RESERVE CAMP	1917 July 1–5		In Bde support – Supplied working parties digging Cable Trenches Assembly trenches	
ZUTKERQUE	6.		Arrived to RENINGHELST, entrained there at 11-30 a.m. for WATTEN then Bde. detrained at 3.30 & marched to billets in ZUTKERQUE.	
	7–16.		Training – Aerodrome "Rubber ground"	
HOPPENNER	17.		Arrived from ZUTKERQUE at 12.15 p.m. – entrained at WORMHOUDT at 4.0 p.m. – Schaut near WIPPENHEK at 11.30 p.m. – marched to CONNAUGHT CAMP.	
CONNAUGHT CAMP	18–21.		Training – resting.	
PALACE CAMP	22.		Marched to PALACE CAMP.	
CHATEAU SEGARD	23.		Marched to CHATEAU SEGARD. M.T. Coxn – arrived 1.15 a.m.	
	24–29.		Supplied carrying parties & my Bn to the forward area – sent Officers & other Ganisers to reconnoitre SANCTUARY WOOD and July.	
ZILLEBEKE BUND	29.		Arrived at ZILLEBEKE BUND – arrived 7.30 p.m.	

WAR DIARY

16th (S) Bn. MANCHESTER REGT.   Army Form C. 2118

INTELLIGENCE SUMMARY
(Erase heading not required.)

VOLUME XXII – July – Page 2.

Place	Date	Hour	Summary of Events and Information	Remarks and references to Appendices
ZILLEBEKE BUND	July 29.		Artillery final preparation for attack.	
	30.		Moved to Assembly positions in SANCTUARY WOOD - In position at 3.0 a.m. 31st inst.	
	31.		Attacked Enemy First trenches CLAPHAM JUNCTION – SURBITON VILLAS – Objective gained – Bn. H.Q. established JACKDAW TRENCH at 6.15 a.m.	SEE APPENDIX I & O.O.
			For report on operations SEE APPENDIX II.	APPENDIX II for report on Operations
			CASUALTIES from mort.	
				Killed	Wounded	Missing	Missing Believed Killed	Missing Believed Wounded	
			Officers	1	10.	1	–	–	For nominal Roll see APPENDIX III.
			O.R.	22	169	35	1	3	
			AWARDS during July. D/7055 C/M SIMPSON. G. awarded Military Medal for showing conspicuous bravery throughout period on five occasions witnessed by several men.	See APPENDIX IV

W. Blake Lt. Col.
Commdg. 16th (S) Bn. Manchester Regt.

WAR DIARY - APPENDIX I.

OPERATION ORDER No. 3.

Reference ZILLEBEKE Map 1/10,000

1. INTENTION and OBJECTIVE

The 90th Brigade will attack the BLACK LINE which runs from J.14.d.5 5 to J.8.c.5 5.

The 16th (S) Bn Manchester Regiment will be on the left of the 90th Brigade and will attack the portion of the BLUE LINE which runs in a N.W. direction from J.13.d.9 9 (CHAPHAM JUNCTION) through SURBITON VILLAS to J.13.b.4 5.

The 17th (S) Bn Manchester Regiment will be in support to the 16th Bn Manchester Regiment and will leap frog over the BLUE LINE and attack the BLACK LINE.

2. METHOD OF ATTACK.

(a) The 18th Bn Manchester Regiment will attack on the right with the 2nd R.S.F. in support.

16th Bn Manchester Regiment will attack on the left with 17th Bn Manchester Regiment in support.

(On our left the 1st Worcestershire Regiment will attack supported by the 2nd East Lancs both Battalions belonging to the 8th Division).

(b) (i) The attack will be made on the leap frog principle.

(ii) The attack will be carried out at dawn.

(iii) The pace of the advance will be 100 yards per 4 minutes.

(iv) There will be a halt of about 30 minutes on the BLUE LINE but the first waves of the 17th Manchester Regiment will leap frog over the BLUE LINE and advance some 200 yards before halting.

(c) The attack on the portion of the BLUE LINE allotted to this Battalion will be carried out in 3 waves each wave consisting of Platoons in 2 lines.

The first wave will advance as far as the line JACKDAW SUPPORT from J.13.c.77.10 to J.13.c.40.88 throwing out in front of the assembly position a screen of 12 men to remain in JACKDAW TRENCH and mop up from J.19.a.05.90 to J.13.c.03.70.

The second wave will advance as far as the line of JACKDAW RESERVE from J.13.d.20.40 to J.13.a.85.17.

The third wave (which will be double the strength of the first and second waves) will advance to the BLUE LINE and will consolidate the position gained there.

Each wave will be responsible for cleaning up dug-outs, strong points and trenches in and behind its objective as & far as the next Company's line.

(d) Bn H.Q. will move from LOVERS WALK to approximately J.13.c.14 after all the 17th Manchester Regt have passed over (about Zero + 30).

3. BOUNDARIES

   Right.
   The boundary between 16th and 18th Manchester Regiments will be:-
   J.13.d.90.90.
   J.13.d.20.40.
   J.13.c.77.10.
   J.19.a.05.90.
   I.24.b.20.70.

   Left.
   The boundary between 16th Manchester Regiment and 1st Bn Worcester Regiment will be:-
   J.13.b.40.50.
   J.13.a.85.17.
   J.13.c.40.88.
   J.13.c.03.80.
   I.18.d.10.30

   Boundaries between Coys forming the 3rd wave:-
   J.13.b.75.26
   J.13.d.05.75.
   J.13.c.50.45
   J.13.c.05.30.
   I.18.d.30.05.

4. DISPOSITION of the Battalion for the attack.

   1st Wave: A Company
   2nd Wave: B Company.
   3rd Wave.   C.Company on the Right.
               D.Company on the left.

5. MACHINE GUNS.

   4 Guns of 90th Machine Gun Coy will follow close behind the 3rd Wave and occupy positions on BLUE LINE in the neighbourhood of CLAPHAM JUNCTION. They will move forward to BLACK LINE close behind rear wave of 17th Manchester Regiment.

6. ASSEMBLY POSITIONS.

   On X day.   Forward area East of LILLE ROAD.

   X/Y night and   WELLINGTON CRESCENT and two trenches
   Y day.   west of it.

   Y/Z night.   Front line Trenches.
                          Bn. H.Q. will be in LOVERS WALK at approximately I.24.b.27

7. SIGNAL COMMUNICATIONS.

(a) TELEPHONIC.

(i) Prior to the attack, Bn H.Q. will be connected to Brigade H.Q from the buried cable which runs from DORMY HOUSE through YEOMANRY POST to H Q 23 (I.24.b.27).

(ii) After the attack. As soon as possible after the attack the Brigade forward station will move forward from H.Q. 23 and establish itself in JACKDAW RESERVE Trench at approximately J.13.d.24 laying D 5 Cable as it goes along.

(iii) N.C.O. in charge of Bn signals will lay line of D.5 Cable and be responsible for its upkeep from Bn H.Q. to Brigade Runner post in JACKDAW AVENUE (approximately J.13.o.72) and tap into wire mentioned in para (ii). Brigade Signalling Officer will issue the Cable.
Company lines will be established as soon as possible and a line run to the Bn. H.Q. on the right (18th Manchester Regiment).

(b) VISUAL.

(i) Brigade visual stations will be established as follows:-
In LOVERS WALK I 24.b.2.5.
In JACKDAW RESERVE about J.13.d.3.4.
(Joint 21st & 90th Brigade station)

(ii) The N.C.O i/c signals will get into touch with Brigade by visual as soon as Bn H.Q. has moved forward to the vicinity of JACKDAW TRENCH (J.13.o.14) and test every half hour.

(iii) 2 signallers will go forward with each of "B" "C" and "D" Coys and establish visual communication with Bn H.Q. as early as possible.

(c) PIGEONS.

2 will be issued to this Battalion.

(d) SIGNALLING STORES as follows will be taken into action:-

4 X 3 Buzzer Unit.
1 D III Fullerphone.
6 D III Telephones
Aeroplane sheet and strips.
2 Lamps for Bn. H.Q and 1 per Coy.
Cable.
Flags
Binoculars
Shutters.

6. SUPPLIES

(a) RATIONS.

One day's rations will be dumped in Assembly Trenches a few days before Zero.

Until Z + 1 day these rations are a reserve. On a Z + 1 day they will be consumed as the rations for the day.

On X day rations will be issued for consumption on Y and Z days as no transport will be allowed to move forward of the Canal on Y/Z night.

(b) WATER.

There are water points at:

ZILLEBEKE LAKE

MAPLE COPSE (This will probably break down through shell fire).

Also wells at CRAB CRAWL dug-outs from which drinking water can be obtained.

About 20 fifty gallon casks will be placed in the Assembly Trenches of the Brigade. Parties will be called for on W/X night to fill these and afterwards guard them.

It must be impressed on all ranks that water must be used sparingly as it may not be possible to get water forward the first day at all.

(c) AMMUNITION.

S.A.A., Grenade and Very Light dump will be in LOVERS WALK at I.24.b.15.70 and will move forward about 2 hours after zero to approximately J.13.c.12.

(d) SALVAGE.

Forward salvage dumps will be established at suitable points and will be clearly marked "SALVAGE DUMP". All ranks returning from the front line for any reason should return articles worth salving to these dumps.

9. STORES TO BE CARRIED.

The following table gives a list of stores, etc. to be carried by Battalions

ITEM. BY WHOM CARRIED.	STORES, DRESS or EQUIPMENT.	REMARKS.
1. Every man.	Rations.-(a) Unconsumed portion of day's ration. (b) 1 Iron Emergency Ration.	
2. Every man.	Ammunition.-(a) 120 rounds S.A.A. (b) 2 Mills Grenades.	Except as in Item 5, Bombs required will be taken over from Div.Bomb store H.26.b.7.6. and detonated when instructed by Brigade.
3. Every man.	Various.-(a) Entrenching Tool, & Helve. (b) 4 Sandbags. (c) Small Box Respirator. (d) P.H.Helmet. (e) Water bottle, full.	Greatcoats will NOT be carried.
4. Each platoon.	12 Shovels. 6 Picks.	Units will be notified when to draw these.
5. Each Bombing Section.	Bombs.-(a) Each thrower 10 Mills Grenades. (b) Each carrier-20 Mills Grenades. (c) Each leader -10 Mills Grenades.	Throwers only carry 50 rounds S.A.A. Every bomber will have a key attached to his wrist.
6. Each Rifle Grenade Section.	Rifle Grenades (a) Each grenadier-10. No 20 or 24. (b) Each grenadier-5 No 23 Rifle Grenades.	The establishment of cups for Mills Rifle Grenades will be evenly distributed between the Bomber Sections. Each man of the Bomber Section will carry 50 rounds Blank Ammunition for firing Rifle Grenade. Grenades required will be taken over from Div.Bomb Store H.26.b.7.6 and detonated when instructed by Bde.
7. Each Platoon.	Wire Cutters Mark V 6. Wire Cutters 4. Wire Cutters, long handled 6. Hedging Gloves.	These stores have been asked for on this scale, but it is doubtful if they will be available.

8. Each man   2 flares (white in tins)   1000 will be issued to the Bn and will be distributed as far as they will go at the rate mentioned.

9. Divided up in each Platoon.   Position Flags. 1 small red and yellow flag.

10. Do   Very Pistol Ammunition.
   2 - 1" and 3 - 1½"
   S.O.S. Colour.

Packs will not be carried in the attack.

Arrangements will be made to store them at the Transport Lines.

10. NUMBER OF OFFICERS & O.R. TO TAKE PART IN ATTACK.

(1) Not more than 20 Officers, excluding the Medical Officer are to go into action with the Battalion.

(2) The following officers will be left behind:-

 (a) Battn. Hdqrs. - Either the C.O. or 2nd in Command.

 (b) Per Company. - Either the Company Commander or the 2nd in Command. Not more than two Company Commanders are to go in with their Companies.

(3) The following "Other Ranks" will be left behind:-

 (a) In Each Battalion

Company Sergeant Majors.	2	
33 per cent Signallers.	10 x	
33 per cent Runners.	13 x	
Gas Instructor.	1	
Bombing Instructor.	1	
Lewis Gun Instructors.	2	
Any other Instructors in special work, such as dug-outs.	3	
	32	32

 (b) In each Company

Sergeant.	1.	
Corporal	1.	
Lance Corporal	1.	
	3	12.

 (c) In each Platoon

Rifle Bomber	1	
Scout & Sniper	1	
Lewis Gunners.	2	
	4	64
		108

x If up to full strength.

(4) The following will be included in the above numbers:-

 (a) Any Officer or O.R. on leave.

 (b) Any N.C.Os detailed as permanent personell at the Divisional Reinforcement Battalion.

 (c) Any Officer or O.R. attending Courses at Schools of Instruction.

(5) The Officers and Other Ranks left behind, with the exception of those attending Courses, will be sent to the advanced Reinforcement Camp (Location to be notified later) with the following exception:-

 (a) 1 Rifle Bomber)
   1 Scout & Sniper) per Platoon
   2 Lewis Gunners)
who will remain at the Battalion Transport Lines.

 (b) The N.C.O's mentioned in para 4 (b) will remain at Corps Reinforcement Camp WILLIAM.

 (c) Orders for any moves are required will be issued by 30th Division Q.

11. MEDICAL

    (a) Regimental Aid Post will be established at I.24.a.7.4 (VINT STREET).
        The Aid Post will move forward to Dug-outs in the German Trenches probably near the Craters in JACKDAW SUPPORT as soon after Zero as is feasible.

    (b) Walking Wounded. The various routes will be "flagged" for walking wounded to collect them at WHITHUIS I.19.d.0 2 fro, which place they will be conveyed by busses and lorries to the Corps Main Dressing Station.

12. DISPOSITION OF PRISONERS and CAPTURED DOCUMENTS.

    (a) An advanced Prisoners of War Cage will be established at CAFE BELGE H.29.b.8.4 to which place Prisoners will be taken by escorts detailed from Bn. H.Q. (A Coy will probably provide the escorts); the strength of each escort will be as follows:-
        Up to 75 Prisoners.   3 men
        From 75 - 150 "   4 men
          " 150 - 250 "   5 men
          " 250 - 350 "   6 men.

    (b) All Prisoners captured by this Bn are to be sent straight to Bn H.Q. under escort provided by the Coys capturing them. After handing them over to the Bn H.Q. the escort from the Coys will rejoin their Coys.
        All ranks will be warned that the above is the procedure for dealing with Prisoners and that any man of the final front Coys proceeding beyond Bn H.Q. with Prisoners is committing a serious offence.

    (c) Direction Boards are being put up at all forward tracks marked with the Div. crest and the letters "P of W" with an arrow.
        O.C. "A" Coy will instruct all his men of this and warn them that if detailed as escorts to Prisoners they should follow these direction boards, otherwise the Prisoners might be handed over to a different Divisional Cage.

    (d) Nothing is to be taken from Prisoners except Arms and explosives unless time can be found to search Officers and N.C.Os for documents and Maps in which case these may be removed, tied in a separate bundle for each prisoner and sent down with the escort to Bn. H.Q.
        NOTE No unnecessary time should be wasted in sending prisoners back.

13. COLLECTION OF INFORMATION, MAPS &c

    (a) All cleaning up Parties are to be carefully instructed to gather up any documents, Maps &c from Dug-outs and forward to Bn. H.Q. as quickly as possible.

    (b) O.C. "A" Coy will detail 2 men to assist the Intelligence Officer. Their duty will be to search as many dug-outs as possible particularly those suspected as being former H.Q. These men will move with Bn. H.Q. and will wear Yellow Arm bands with "BQ INTEL" marked in black on them. They will be provided with Sandbags marked in the same way.
        These Sandbags when filled will be sent to the Divl. Intelligence Officer at the Divl Cage by the escorts to prisoners or by lightly wounded men.

(c) **Writing of Reports.** These must be concise, clear and time and position stated.

A special message form in the form of the Active Service postcard will be issued having a map printed on it. When sending reports positions should be marked clearly on the map.

(d) **Maps to be carried.** In addition to the special forms mentioned in the preceding para, maps showing the ground to be covered in the attack to the scale of 1/10,000, will be issued to all Officers.

These maps will be the only maps to be carried during the attack. Officers will not make any notes on them which might prove useful to the enemy excepting when sending messages back on the special form.

14. COMMUNICATION TRENCHES &c

(a) **In our lines.**

(i) There are only two communication trenches in the Divisional Area, VINCE STREET and ZILLEBEKE STREET.

(ii) On Z day these will both be reserved for OUT traffic i.e. from the front.
All traffic towards the front will be over the open.

(iii) After Z day, some modification of this order will probably be required but positive orders will be sent.

(b) **In the enemy lines.**

The following communication trenches will be cleared and kept open for use in the 30th Brigade area:-
Opening up JAP AVENUE and trench leading West from it so that a continuous trench will run from JACKDAW RESERVE at J.13.d.25.35. via CLAPHAM JUNCTION and JAP AVENUE to the BLACK LINE.

(c) **Notice Boards.**

Notice Boards to mark all enemy trenches and specially the communication trenches to be kept open will be prepared and placed in position under the orders of the C.R.E.

(d) **Infantry Tracks.**

Infantry tracks will be allotted as follows:-

No 1 Track to 30th Division for IN traffic (towards trenches).
No 2 " 30th Division for OUT traffic.
No 3 " 18th Division for IN traffic.
No 4 " 18th Division for OUT traffic.
No 4 " 18th and 30th) (walking wounded
          Division   ) for (OUT traffic.

ARTILLERY BARRAGE.

(1) (a) The barrage will be put down on the enemy's front line at Zero and will remain there from Zero to Zero plus 3 mins.

It will advance over the first 100 yards in 3 minutes
"   "   "   "   next "   " " 3½   "
"   "   "   "   "   "   " " 3   "

After this it will advance at a uniform pace of 100 yards in 4 minutes.

(b) It will cross the BLUE LINE as follows:-

Between CLAPHAM JUNCTION & N. of SURBITON VILLAS at Zero plus 30 minutes.
Between CLAPHAM JUNCTION and JASPER AVENUE at Zero plus 38 minutes.

(c) It will continue to advance 300 yards beyond the BLUE LINE, when a protective barrage will be established at Zero plus 46 mins. Between CLAPHAM JUNCTION and Northern Boundary of 90th Infantry Brigade, and at Zero plus 54 mins. from CLAPHAM JUNCTION to Southern Brigade Boundary.

(d) It will continue to advance again at Zero plus 1 hour 45 mins. and will cross the BLACK LINE at Zero plus 1 hour 50 minutes except just east of INVERNESS COPSE where it will cross at Zero plus 2 hour 47 minutes.

(e) It will continue to advance 300 yards beyond the BLACK LINE where a protective barrage will be established at Zero plus 1 hour 55 minutes.

(f) It will commence to advance again at Zero plus 6 hours 24 minutes, and will cross the GREEN LINE at Zero plus 6 hours 40 minutes.

(2) The ordinary rate of fire will be 2 rounds per gun per minute except when the barrage piles on a trench, the rate will then be 4 rounds per gun per minute during the 4 minutes immediately preceding the lift off.

Troops will be warned to look out for the increased rate of fire, and to get as close to the barrage as possible, preparing to rush the trench as soon as the artillery lifts.

(3) (a) During protective barrages, the rate will be ½ round per minute for 30 minutes, and then dying down to occasional rounds to mark the protective line.

(b) During the last 8 mins. of the protective barrage in front of the BLUE and BLACK LINES, the rate will be increased to 4 rounds per gun per minute.
All ranks will be warned about this.

16. COLLECTING OF STORES:

After the GREEN LINE has been captured O.C. "B" Company will be called upon to provide a Carrying Party of 100 Other Ranks with Officers.

On receipt of orders from Bn. H.Q. this party will proceed to collect the enemy's stores, wire, stakes and entrenching tools.

These stores will be dumped at the South West Corner of INVERNESS COPSE about J.14.c.4.4.

Amendments to O.O. No 3.

Para 8 (a). Page 4.

The Rations mentioned will be for consumption on Z+2 day, not Z+1 as therein stated.

Para 7. SIGNAL COMMUNICATIONS. Page 3.

Add: (e) Special Message Rockets will be issued to send back important messages.

(f) O.C. "A" Coy will detail 1 N.C.O. and 3 men who will establish a relay post at the BEAK (I.24.b. 9 7). This party will carry 1 stand and 4 rockets.
      This party will keep a continuous look out for messages coming from the direction of the front line and immediately a rocket lands it will be collected, the message taken by the N.C.O in charge and placed in another rocket and fired to the next relay post which will be at approximately I.24.b. 2 7.

(g) As the supply of rockets is very limited messages sent thereby should only be of a very important nature such as:
    (i) Capture of objective.
    (ii) Failure of capture objective and reason of failure.
    (iii) Hostile counter attack.
      All messages sent by rockets must be repeated by Runner, phone, or visual.

(h) The Officer of A Coy who was present at the demonstration of these Rockets will carefully instruct the N.C.O. and men detailed in
    (i) use of rocket.
    (ii) method of firing.

   Reference page 9, para 14 (d) INFANTRY TRACKS.
      Tracks will now be renumbered as follows:-
      For No 1 read No 11.
       "   2   "   10
       "   3. "   9.
       "   5. "   7.
       "   4   "   8.

Addressed to all recipients of O.O. No 3.

WAR DIARY - APPENDIX II

16th (S) Bn Manchester Regiment.

REPORT on OPERATIONS (31. 7. 17.).

BACK Bn were E and clear of STANLEY STREET by 1.15 am. They gradually took up their assembly positions SANCTUARY WOOD found to be extremely difficult for large body of troops to move about in but assembly not discovered by Germans and everybody in correct position before Zero, touch being gained with BAWL on the right, but unable to discover ARTFUL on left.

At Zero (3.50 am) Bn commenced to close up and advance under barrage no hostile barrage encountered, about half a dozen casualties to our 1st wave by being too close to own barrage fire.

At 4.15 am. Bn H.Q. who advanced behind 3rd wave were established in JACKDAW TRENCH.

"A" Coy whose objective was JACKDAW SUPPORT gained their line about 4.15 am encountering practically no opposition, a few Boches who were holding this trench put up a half hearted fight, but these were immediately dealt with. Touch was gained with BAWL on right, but not with ARTFUL on left.

"B" Coy reached JACKDAW RESERVE about 4.30 am. Some of B Coy were here went off to the right and instead of entering JACKDAW SWITCH got to STIRLING CASTLE stables, the Coy Commander being killed just before reaching the stables.

About a dozen men reached STIRLING CASTLE stables. On arrival of BALD and BAWL a withdrawal to the left was made by BACK. Practically no opposition from JACKDAW RESERVE - Boche ran away.

C Company on right reached CLAPHAM JUNCTION on heels of barrage, and entered it without difficulty. A few Boches were met with in the tunnel; the CLAPHAM JUNCTION area was badly damaged by our own artillery fire, and many dug-outs blown in. The right platoons pushed over the road and took up their position on BLUE LINE. Hostile machine gun fire caused a certain number of casualties, the Coy Commander succeeded in knocking out a hostile machine gun by a shot from his rifle. Touch was gained by C Coy with BALD on right and with right of D Coy BACK at J.13.b. 5 1.

The left of D Coy with about 15 men and an officer from C Coy missed the barrage and were only able to make their way over the bend of the YPRED-MENIS road with difficulty.

The units were very mixed up at this point, and men of about 8 different Bns forced their way over the road between 5.15 am and 6 am. About 30 - 40 prisoners were captured with machine gun and trench mortar amongst dug-outs and trenches N of bend.

The barrage being missed hostile machine guns were a great source of difficulty and held up the advance. Touch was gained with Mr PRICE and Mr BARTON of ARTFUL at this point i.e. J.13.b. 0 4.

After cleaning and clearing the dug-out area N of the bend in YPRES MENIN road a strong point was consolidated on the right about J.13.b.2 4. The strong point dug commanded the ground lying around SURBITON VILLAS and up to the high ground around CLAPHAM JUNCTION.

A large number of men under the command of Captain ORR (RABBLE) reached the area lying around J.13.b.14.

SUMMARY of Impressions of the Attack made
upon immediate Front of RACK.

1. No hostile shelling encountered in forward assembly position.

2. Very great difficulty in advancing through SANCTUARY WOOD, but no opposition met with as long as troops kept close enough to barrage.

3. The difficulties of SANCTUARY WOOD were responsible for serious losses of direction.

4. The Pause on the BLUE LINE should have been of longer duration before proceeding to attack BLACK LINE.

5. Communications very bad throughout the battle, the small card maps issued not quite distinct enough, and may have been a minor cause for ignorance of correct positions attained by troops.

Between 4 - 6 pm 31st inst Boche aeroplane was flying very low and noting position taken up by infantry.

(Sd) W. ELSTOB. Lieut- Colonel.

WAR DIARY - APPENDIX III

16th (S) Bn Manchester Regiment.

CASUALTY LIST. BELGIUM

Capt. E. BRODRICK. 31.7.17. Killed in Action

A/27034 Pte HORROCKS	22.7.17.	D/33164 Pte BELFIELD H.	27.7.17.
D/37934 " DOCKERTY J.	27.7.17.	D/51081 Pte WARD W.A.	27.7.17.
D/51061 Pte ROBINSON J.	27.7.17.	D/245106 Pte GARNER W.	27.7.17.
C/36833 Pte SMITH A.A.	28.7.17.	C/42290 Pte ALLPORT F.J.	28.7.17.
A/303012 L/Cpl DAVIES J.H.	31.7.17.	A/51028 Pte Grover A.	31.7.17.
B/42297 Pte HEAP H.	31.7.17.	B/245126 Pte HUGHES R.J.	31.7.17.
B/33644 Pte RAWCLIFFE W.	31.7.17.	B/245129 Pte HIGHAM	30.7.17.
C/6769 Sgt LAWRENSON F.J.	30.7.17.	43076 L/Cpl GEORGE A.	30.7.17.
C/43071 L/Cpl BUTLER J.E.	30.7.17.	C/51035 Pte HAMSHAW W.H.	30.7.17.
D/7154 Sgt STUTTARD C.A.	31.7.17.	D/49961 Pte FRANCE E.	31.7.17.
D/7071 L/Cpl WYCHERLEY	31.7.17		
D/51034 Pte HUMPHREY F.	2.8.17.		

Wounded in Action

A/245111 Pte GREENHALGH	24.7.17.	A/48585 Pte MILLWARD	24.7.17.
B/203158 Pte FARNELL M.	25.7.17.	B/245092 Pte CHURCH J.	25.7.17.
D/51037 Pte HAYNES H.	25.7.17.	C/202955 Pte JOB F.	26.7.17.
A/40884 Pte WATTS A.V.	23.7.17.	B/30249 Pte CASEY T.	25.7.17.
D/41879 Pte MORTON W.J.	27.7.17.	C/48153 Pte LATHAM J.	27.7.17.
D/40823 Pte MURPHY G.	27.7.17.	D/42301 Pte LOMAS F.	27.7.17.
D/51070 Pte TILLEY W.	27.7.17.	D/45487 Pte STOTT E.	27.7.17.
D/38104 Pte DEARNALLY	27.7.17.	D/41875 L/Cpl LOFTHOUSE	27.7.17.
D/33487 Pte DOBSON W.R.	27.7.17.	D/51075 Pte WATSON	27.7.17.
B/5636 L/Cpl JOWLE R.		B/37655 Pte STOCKTON L.	
(At Duty)	27.7.17.	(At Duty)	27.7.17.
D/2938 Pte WOODCOCK R.	27.7.17.	C/19373 L/Cpl DUNBAR	28.7.17.
C/33567 Pte DAWSON C.	28.7.17.	C/35473 Pte SHARPLES E.	28.7.17.
C/45459 Pte COKAYNE P.	28.7.17.	C/203170 Pte BUCKLEY D.	28.7.17.
C/7567 Pte LEE R.	28.7.17.	C/32622 Pte LLOYD W.	28.7.17.
C/51039 Pte HOLMES F.	28.7.17.	C/277767 Pte GUSTAFF	28.7.17.
C/29141 Pte DOVER J.B.	28.7.17.	B/43005 Pte CLARKE G.H.	29.7.17.
C/43087 L/Cpl ROBINSON H.	29.7.17.	C/41853 Pte ALLEN H.T.	29.7.17.
C/51382 Pte MOLYNEUX	29.7.17.	C/51280 Pte BALL R.J.	29.7.17.
A/7158 Sgt THOMPSON E.	29.7.17.	D/30095 L/Sgt BROOKE-FOX H.	29.7.17.
D/49004 Pte HOOPER H.	29.7.17.	C/37561 L/Cpl LANSLEY J.	29.7.17.
C/32926 Pte WHITEHEAD	29.7.17.	C/48961 Pte DANIELS	29.7.17.
C/49620 Pte HOWARD L.	29.7.17.	C/2308 Pte LYNCH J.	31.7.17.
A/33982 Cpl ALLSOPP W.	31.7.17.	A/41617 L/Sgt Casey G.H.	31.7.17.
A/13548 Cpl ALLOTT A.	31.7.17.	A/20230 L/Cpl HARGREAVES R	31.7.17.
A/16675 L/Cpl WHITEHEAD T.	31.7.17.	A/6250 L/Cpl GRESTY A	31.7.17.
A/51068 Pte TAYLOR R.W.	31.7.17.	A/40854 Pte REVILL E.	31.7.17.
A/27316 Pte HARVEY J.H.	31.7.17.	A/51269 Pte SAWKILL J.C.	31.7.17.
A/32514 Pte MUTTON J.	31.7.17.	A/302879 Pte JONES A.	31.7.17.
A/245153 Pte LEAK R.	31.7.17.	A/25713 Pte STANDRING F.	31.7.17.
A/49659 Pte ATKINSON H	31.7.17.	A/48566 Pte YARWOOD H.	31.7.17.
A/36595 Pte OLIVER G.W.	31.7.17.	A/245135 Pte HELME R.	31.7.17.
A/49381 Pte LOWE W.	31.7.17.	A/51053 Pte MARVESLEY J.	31.7.17.
A/51082 Pte PARKER C.J.	31.7.17.	A/245097 Pte DAVIES J.W.	31.7.17.
A/51045 Pte KIRBY A.O.	31.7.17.	A/302774 Pte CUSACK E.	31.7.17.
A/18187 Pte BRADLEY H.	31.7.17.	A/6235 L/Cpl DEAVILLE A	31.7.17.
B/43007 Pte HAYTON J.	31.7.17.	B/7374 Sgt GLEAV E.	31.7.17.
B/250569 Sgt CORMACK R.L.	31.7.17.	B/202190 Pte FIELDING P.	31.7.17.
B/35426 L/Cpl LEWIS B.	31.7.17.	B/28901 Pte BERRY J.	31.7.17.
B/41835 Pte JEFFRIES A.E.	31.7.17.	B/42298 Pte JACKSON A.	31.7.17.
B/41836 Pte KENT G.W.	31.7.17.	B/42303 Pte MATTHEWS T.M.	31.7.17.
B/40868 Pte SALMON J.C.	31.7.17.	B/39445 Pte McGUIRE H.	31.7.17.
R/43008 Sgt LEECH R.	31.7.17.	B/39647 Cpl OSBALDESTON W.	31.7.17.
B/5595 L/Cpl ATKINS A	31.7.17.	B/48765 Pte GRIFFITHS	31.7.17.
B/6497 Pte HALLETT E.	31.7.17.	B/36542 Pte QUALEY P.	31.7.17.
B/34061 Pte STORER G.H.	31.7.17.	B/29431 L/Cpl LANCASTER C	31.7.17.
B/35853 L/Cpl MASON	31.7.17.	B/6346 Pte BROUGHTON A	31.7.17.
B/252648 Pte CHUBB A	31.7.17.	B/245104 Pte FISHER W.	31.7.17.
B/42307 Pte SEAMAN J.	31.7.17.	B/252615 Pte ADAMSON H.	31.7.17.
F1048 Sgt Barker.	31.7.17.		

CASUALTIES contd. sheet 2.

Officers   Wounded in Action.

Lieut. W.S. KIDD. M.O.,R.A.M.C.att:	27.7.17.	Revd R. PARK. Chaplain attached.	27.7.17.
2/Lieut A.A.BOWES	31.7.17.	Captain A.G.SHAW	31.7.17.
2/Lieut S.HALL	31.7.17.	2/Lieut T.HANSON	31.7.17.
2/Lieut R.A.WHITTLE	31.7.17.	2/Lieut J.OLLERENSHAW	31.7.17.
2/Lieut B. NAYLOR.	30.7.17.		

Missing.

2/Lieut J.C.JACKSON.   31.7.17.

Wounded slightly at Duty.

2/Lieut E.N.ASHE   31.7.17.

N.C.Os & men.   Wounded in action

B/203158 Pte FARRELL H.C.	31.7.17.	B/245123 Pte HOLDEN J.	31.7.17
B/250746 Pte RUSHTON J.	31.7.17.	B/43005 Pte CLARKE G.	31.7.17.
B/252548 Pte WILDE W.G.	31.7.17.	C/40915 Sgt HUGHES J.K.	31.7.17.
C/246732 Cpl MULLEN J.	31.7.17.	C/6716 L/Cpl Bell A.	31.7.17.
C/38696 L/Cpl NUTTALL H.	31.7.17.	C/35641 L/Cpl LEE A.	31.7.17.
C/48787 Pte HARRISON F.	31.7.17.	C/276097 Pte SHARROCK S.W.	31.7.17
C/35097 Pte OGDEN F.	31.7.17.		
C/51026 Pte FARENDEN J.	31.7.17.	C/51033 Pte HUNT C.J.	31.7.17.
C/51033 Pte GREEN G.	31.7.17.	C/7578 Sgt JOHNSON H.	31.7.17.
C/6802 Sgt SCHAEFER C.	31.7.17.	D/7004 Sgt HOLMES A.	31.7.17.
D/32336 L/Sgt HEATHFIELD	31.7.17	D/16352 Cpl ASHWORTH A	31.7.17.
D/245121 Cpl HODKINSON W	31.7.17.	D/41873 Cpl JOHNSON W	31.7.17
D/7622 L/Cpl LONGDEN W.	31.7.17.	D/37622 L/Cpl Portman F.	31.7.17
D/23184 L/Cpl SEDDON C.	31.7.17.	D/43099 L/Cpl CLEMENTS A	31.7.17
D/7292 L/Cpl BOSTWICK	31.7.17.	D/3285 L/Cpl AUSTIN	31.7.17.
D/40806 L/Cpl STIRLAND W.	31.7.17.	D/41867 L/Cpl HART W.	31.7.17.
D/245101 Pte EGAN J.	31.7.17.	D/42299 Pte KAVANAGH M.	31.7.17.
D/245105 Pte GIBSON W.	31.7.17.	D/35161 Pte & FOWDEN	31.7.17.
D/36625 Pte CHADWICK H.	31.7.17	D/42291 Pte COWPERTHWAITE	31.7.17
D/52063 Pte RYECROFT A.	31.7.17.	D/51041 Pte HOLLOWAY A	31.7.17.
D/48780 Pte HOLT A.	31.7.17.	D/6953 Pte BARRINGTON	31.7.17.
D/245127 Pte HUGHES W.J.	31.7.17.	D/7007 Pte HUGHES R.	31.7.17.
D/34210 Pte MCCORMICK F.	31.7.17.	D/34298 Pte GOWRIE	31.7.17.
C/48961 Pte DANIELS	31.7.17.	C/49620 Pte HOWARD L.	31.7.17.
D/46651 Pte BROOKS R.	31.7.17.	C/41858 Pte ENGLAND.	31.7.17.
C/202165 Pte CLAY	31.7.17.	D/51022 Pte DUNMAIN A	31.7.17
C/41853 Pte ALLEN H.T.	29.7.17.	B/32362 Pte BATTMAN A.	31.7.17.
B/32083 Pte CORSON H.	31.7.17.	A/302967 Pte PHILLIPS E.	31.7.17
C/51280 Pte HALL R.J.	29.7.17.	C/43087 L/Cpl ROBINSON H	29.7.17
A/49124 Pte OGDEN F.	31.7.17.	B/45077 Pte HOLMES H.	31.7.17.
B/35483 Pte ROBERTS W.	31.7.17.	B/245107 Pte GUY J.	31.7.17.
B/245141 Pte JONES H.	31.7.17.	B/245108 Pte GRAHAM W	31.7.17.
B/245148 Pte KING C.W.	31.7.17.	B/34252 Pte WILD H.	31.7.17.
B/29623 Pte DAVIES J.N.	31.7.17.	C/39932 Pte HIGHTON J.	31.7.17.
C/43077 Pte GRAY G.W.	31.7.17.	C/7293 Pte WALKER G.W.	31.7.17.
D/41872 Pte HOZIER A.D.	31.7.17.	A/302988 Pte KAYE J.	31.7.17.
A/51042 Pte INNS W.	31.7.17.	B/18600 Pte HARRISON G.W.	31.7.17
B/245100 Pte DONE G.	31.7.17.	B/245102 Pte ELLISON J.E.	31.7.17.
B/277237 Pte KNOWLES F.	31.7.17.	B/200440 Pte PARKER C.	31.7.17
B/7056 L/Cpl SMITH H.F.	31.7.17.	C/51010 Pte CORY C.	31.7.17.
C/49448 Pte PARTON	31.7.17.	D/48661 Pte GREEN	31.7.17.
D/42146 Pte HALLIGAN J.H.	31.7.17.	D/245140 Pte INMAN D	31.7.17
D/51073 Pte FURNOCK A.	31.7.17.	B/27419 Pte DAWSON F	31.7.17
		D/35455 Pte CROLLA F	31.7.17
D/49025 Pte BERRY D	2.8.17	D/49016 Pte BICKERTON W	2.8.17
D/51059 Pte PETTIT H.	2.8.17	A/245138 Pte HOLMES	2.8.17
A/48874 Pte AINSWORTH	2.8.17.		
D/51058 Pte PETTIT A.	31.7.17		

CASUALTIES Contd (Sheet 3).

Missing

D/6991 L/Cpl GRIFFITHS A.	28.7.17.	D/40824 Pte MILLS R. 31.7.17.
D/42304 Pte MORGAN J.	31.7.17.	D/48669 Pte PARTT W. 31.7.17.
D/71080 Pte WADE J.	31.7.17.	D/29107 Pte JACKSON W. 31.7.17
D/51049 Pte LIGO F.	31.7.17.	D/33356 Pte MILLS S. 31.7.17.
D/25099 Pte PEARSON J.	31.7.17.	D/42306 Pte PADFIELD F. 31.7.17.
D/36838 Pte ROBINSON A.	31.7.17.	D/51069 Pte TURNER H 31.7.17
D/51074 Pte WILLIAMS F.	31.7.17.	A/325997 Pte DANIELS H.K 31.7.17
A/51268 Pte SHAW E.	31.7.17.	
A/49740 Pte BROMLEY A	31.7.17.	A/40871 Pte TOLLEY W. 31.7.17
B/201517 Cpl NEWALL J.	31.7.17.	B/42295 Pte GREEN O. 31.7.17
B/7221 Pte GRIFFIN M.	31.7.17.	B/41826 Pte GILBERT A. 31.7.17
B/245128 Pte HORNBY L.	31.7.17.	R/245155 Pte HALL R. 31.7.17
B/32631 Pte GREENHALGH J.F.	31.7.17.	B/4358 L/Cpl BRIDSON 31.7.17
B/252598 Pte BENNETT G.	31.7.17.	B/41839 Pte MERRIMAN A.P.31.7.17
B/40848 Pte PEARSON J.E.S.	31.7.17.	B/48972 Pte COLE J. 31.7.17
C/275982 Sgt BOWDEN W.	31.7.17	C/11773 L/Cpl COOKE W.K 31.7.17.
C/51005 Pte BROWNING F.	31.7.17.	D/40906 Pte BRADBURY E.31.7.17
D/45322 Pte HYDE J.	31.7.17.	D/245131 Pte HOWARTH R 31.7.17
C/47470 Pte SIMMONS	31.7.17.	C/51286 Pte STUTTER W.E.31.7.17
D/34895 Pte WOODS	31.7.17.	

Missing believed Wounded

B/35594 L/Cpl ELLIS A.   31.7.17.   B/6646 Sgt MC MINN W.J. 31.7.17
B/201360 Pte SIMPSON J.   31.7.17.

Missing believed Killed

C/18460 Cpl BRADBURY J.   31.7.17

SUMMARY.

	Killed.	Wounded.	Missing.	Missing believed W.
Officers.	1	10	1	
Other Ranks.	22	188	38	3.

Missing believed Killed
1 O.R.

WAR DIARY

APPENDIX IV

AWARDS for month of JULY 1917

D/7055   Cpl SIMPSON G.   Awarded MILITARY MEDAL for Gallantry in the Field.

   Authority IInd Corps No 2/H.R.30/12 dated 29.6.17.

VOLUME XXII.

SECRET

WAR DIARY
FOR THE MONTH OF AUGUST
16TH (S) BATTALION, MANCHESTER REGIMENT.

September 3rd 1917.   ....Lieut-Colonel
                                       Commanding 16th Bn Manchester Regiment

Army Form C. 2118

WAR DIARY
16TH S. Bn. MANCHESTER RGT.
or
INTELLIGENCE SUMMARY
(Erase heading not required.)

VOLUME XXII - AUGUST - Page 1.

Place	Date	Hour	Summary of Events and Information	Remarks and references to Appendices
	1917			
CHATEAU SEGARD	Aug. 1.		Relieved by 2nd BEDS. in YPRES-MENIN RD. sector near HOOGE, & marched to CHATEAU SEGARD.	
DICKEBUSCH	2.		Arrived at Camp near DICKEBUSCH.	
WIPPENHOEK	3.		Moved by 'bus to Billets in WIPPENHOEK (EAST AREA)	
EECKE	4.		Marched to camp in EECKE AREA (near STEENVOORDE).	
	5-6.		Cleaning up - Resting.	
COURTE-CROIX	7.		Marched to Billets at COURTE-CROIX (Near CAESTRE).	
	8-9.		Training.	
BERTHEN	10.		Marched to camp E. of BERTHEN.	
	11-21		Training.	
KEMMEL	22.		Marched to camp near KEMMEL.	
	23-24		Training.	
MESSINES	25.		Relieved 15th Bn. A.I.F. in MESSINES SUPPORT. - Relief complete 9.0 p.m.	
TRENCHES	29.		Relieved 13th Bn. A.I.F. in MESSINES TRENCHES - Relief complete 1.0 a.m. 30th.	
	30.		Dispositions: Left D.Co. Centre B.Co. Right A.Co. Reserve C.Co.	
	31.		Quiet day.	
			Casualties for month	See APPENDIX I
			Honours & Awards for month	APPENDIX II
				APPENDIX III

War Diary- Appendix I

LIST OF CASUALTIES AUGUST 1917

MESSINES, BELGIUM.

D/6712 R.Q.M.S. ALLEN H.   Wounded in Action 31. 8. 17.

A/11292 Pte TABBRON R.   "   "   31. 8. 17.

A/36626 Pte CORRIGAN E   "   "   31. 8. 17.

A/23095 Pte CAIRNS   "   "   31. 8. 17.
                                           slightly remained at Duty

WAR DIARY. APPENDIX III

CASUALTY LIST FOR JULY.   Corrections.

D/40981.	Pte FRANCE E.	Reported Killed in Action now reported Wounded in Action 31.7.17.
A/40871	Pte TOLLEY W.	Reported Missing in Action now reported Killed in Action 31.7.17.
D/6991	L/Cpl GRIFFITHS A.	Reported Missing in Action now reported Wounded in Action 31.7.17.
D/51049	Pte LIGO	Reported Missing in Action now reported Wounded in Action 31.7.17.
A/49790	Pte BLOMLEY A	Reported Missing in Action now reported Killed in Action 31.7.17.
B/32631	Pte GREENHALGH J	Reported Missing in Action now reported at Duty from F.A.
B/4358	L/Cpl BRIDSON	Reported Missing in Action now reported not Missing.
B/6646	Sgt McMINN W.	Reported Missing in Action now reported Killed in Action 31.7.17.
D/48669	Pte PARTT W.	Reported Missing in Action now reported Wounded in Action 31.7.17.
D/29107	Pte JACKSON W	Reported Missing in Action now reported Not Missing
D/42306	Pte PADFIELD	Reported Missing in Action now reported Not Missing.
D/36838	Pte ROBINSON A.	Reported Missing in Action now reported Wounded in Action.
D/51069	Pte TURNER	Reported Missing in Action now reported Killed in Action.
D/49006	Pte BRADBURY	Reported Missing in Action now reported Not Missing.
D/45322	Pte HYDE	Reported Missing in Action now reported Not Missing.
C/7578	Sgt JOHNSON H.	Reported Wounded in Action now reported Killed in Action.
B/40848	Pte PEARSON J.E.S.	Reported Missing in Action now reported Wounded in Action.
	2/Lieut J. C. JACKSON.	Reported Missing believed Killed now reported Killed in Action.

VOLUME XXIII

SECRET

WAR DIARY
FOR THE MONTH OF SEPTEMBER
16th BATTALION MANCHESTER REGIMENT.

October 2nd 1917.   ....R.E.Roberts........Major
                                     Commanding 16th Bn Manchester Regiment.

WAR DIARY
INTELLIGENCE SUMMARY
(Erase heading not required.)

Army Form C. 2118

16th (S) Bn. MANCHESTER Regt.

VOLUME XXIII - page 1
SEPTEMBER

Place	Date	Hour	Summary of Events and Information	Remarks & references Appendices
TRENCHES	1917 Sept. 1.		In MESSINES Trenches. Relieved by 9th K.R.R. (60th) - Relief complete 12.20 a.m.	
	2.		Arrived at camp near KEMMEL.	
	3.		Supplied Working Parties in WYTSCHAETE Sector — Men wore unshaved - Trench	
	6-10.		Relieved 17th Mchstr. Regt. in support in Q Right Sub-sector.	
	11.		Supplied working parties in Right Sub-sector (WYTSCHAETE) Relief complete 9.30 p.m.	
WYTSCHAETE	12-19.		Relieved 17th K.R.R. in Left Bde Support Sub-sector. Relief complete 10.30 p.m	
TRENCHES	20.		Relieved 17th K.L.R. in Right Sub-sector, Left side. — C. & in reserve.	
	21.		Dispositions:- A & B n/Coys. Relief on Right — D & B in support — A. Coy.	
	22.		A Coy relieved Left 2 Pints of B. Coy.	
	26.		Re-distribution of B D. Sectors. — 16th Bn Mchstr Regt (less D Coy) withdrawn to	
	27.		Support Posn. — Bn. Hd. Den in Wood. A.Coy RAVINE Wood — B. & E EGGERIEN FARM.	
			C to ROSE WOOD.	
IMMELHILL	30.		Relieved by 2nd Leffe Regt. — Relief complete 10.40 p.m & marched to KEMMEL	See Appendix I
CAMP.			HILL CAMP.	
			CASUALTIES for month. Killed. Wounded.	
			O.R. — 7 33 (4 of whom since died of wounds).	
			— 4 Died of Wounds.	

R.E. Roberts. MAJOR
Comd'g 16th (S) Bn. MANCHESTRs

September WAR DIARY
Appendix I.

16th (S) Bn MANCHESTER REGIMENT.

CASUALTIES. BELGIUM. September.

Killed in Action

B/35459 Pte BLOOD (Accidental).	3. 9. 17.
C/51067 Pte STAFFERTON W.	12. 9. 17.
B/40858 Pte RANDALL G.	12. 9. 17.
C/6735 Sgt DAVIES H.	22. 9. 17.
D/26728 L/Cpl HARRISON J.	22. 9. 17.
D/377795 Pte HAMER J.	22. 9. 17.
C/27093 L/Cpl QUANN J.	28. 9. 17.

Wounded in Action

A/6330 Pte WOMBY T.	2. 9. 17.
C/51027 Pte EATON A.H.	6. 9. 17.
C/49013 Pte PARKE A	12. 9. 17.
B/303667 Pte SIMPSON J.	6. 9. 17.
B/29229 Pte GREENALL F.	20. 9. 16
A/31361 Pte WALKER.	20. 9. 16
B/7030 Sgt LAWTON R.	22. 9. 17.
B/6439 Pte TOLLITT.	"
B/245093 Pte DACRE	"
D/17424 L/Cpl MAY	"
D/40823 Pte MURPHY	"
D/51041 Pte HOLLOWAY	"
D/7242 C.S.M. MATHER A.	"
B/36960 L/Cpl FAIRHURST.	"
B/29778 Pte WAINWRIGHT	"
C/13698 Pte CROSBY R.	" Died of Wounds 22nd
D/25169 Pte QUINN	"
D/42301 Pte LOMAS	"
D/51051 Pte MAHER	"
A/43031 L/Cpl MALLINSON.	" Died of Wounds 25th
A/43048 Pte HIGGINS.	"
A/245109 Pte GORST.	24. 9. 17
A/245136 Pte HOLDEN.	"
B/45339 Pte NEWTON	26. 9. 17.
D/40844 Pte POOLE C.	"
D/42294 Pte FURBER.	" Died of Wounds 26th
D/329381 L/Cpl GARNER.	"
D/27021 Pte SCOTT H.	28. 9. 17
C/51004 Pte BOYSON F.	28. 9. 17. Died of Wounds
B/251331 Cpl FARROLL W.H.	27.9.17 29.9.17.
C/51019 Pte DRIVER J.W.	29. 9. 17.
D/42281 Pte YONGE G.E.	29. 9. 17.
A/6350 Pte BURKE.	30. 9. 17.

16th Bn Manchester Regiment.

List of Honours and Awards for August 1917.

2/Lieut R.A. Whittle	Awarded MILITARY CROSS	Auth D.R.O 2981 Dated 21.8.17
2/Lieut W.E.J. Hall.	-do-.	do.
A40890 Sgt Pressley P.	Awarded MILITARY MEDAL	Auth D.R.O 2981 Dated 21.8.17.
A1048 L/Sgt W.T Baiber.	do.	Auth D.R.O 2986 Dated 29.8.17.
A302461 Pte W Warlow.	do.	do.
A12944. L/Cpl Hulbert. S	do.	do.
B29229. Pte F Greenall.	do.	do.
C29017 L/Cpl W Thompson.	do.	do.
C6762 Cpl S Irlam.	do.	do.
C43040 L/Cpl J Cox.	do.	do.
C6835 L/Sgt S Crompton.	do.	do.
C23036 Pte Woolley. T	do.	do.
C38002 L/Sgt H Mullin.	do.	do.
D6988 Cpl Foster. J .	do.	do.
D7345. Pte H. Elsworth.	do.	do.
D7091. L/Cpl A. Coleman.	do.	do.

WO 24

SECRET

WAR DIARY.

16th Bn Manchester Regiment.

VOLUME XXIV

OCTOBER.1917.

W51/Lt. Lieut. Colonel.
Commanding 16th Bn Manchester Regiment.

WAR DIARY or INTELLIGENCE SUMMARY

Army Form C. 2118

10R(S) Bn Manchester Regt.
Volume XIV - Page 1
October

Place	Date	Hour	Summary of Events and Information	Remarks and references to Appendices
KEMMEL HILL CAMP	Oct 1911 Oct 11		Training. Relieved 18th Hampshires in Right Bde battalion support area.	
WYTSCHAETE TRENCHES	11-16 16		Supplied working parties in Right Bde battalion support area (WYTSCHAETE) and R.S.F. in left sub sector. Relief complete 9-45 p.m. Right Bde. Relieved by 2nd Bn Yorkshire Regt. Relief complete 10-15 p.m.	
DAYLIGHT CORNER CAMP	20 20-29 7 29		Marched to Daylight Corner Camp. Renewed Drill Camp. Battalion engaged on making instruments for Winter. Relieved 2nd R.S.F. in Right Bde Support area (WYTSCHAETE)	See Appendix I
			CASUALTIES for month.	
			KILLED WOUNDED OFF 1 (Lt. Galloway) OR. 9 1 (at duty).	

W. Elsden Colonel
Commdg 10R (S) Bn Manchester Regt.

16th Bn Manchester Regiment. Appendix 1.

Casualty List. BELGIUM October.1917.

2/Lieutenant Galloway J.L.   Wounded in Action 14.10.17.

B41842 Pte Puddey A.A.   do.   Do.
A245135. " Helme. R.   do.   16.10.17.
C51024. "   Eales. A.E.   do.   do.
B25339 L/C Ravenscroft.   do.   17.10.17.
                              (Accidentally).
B43016. Cpl Patient. A.   Wounded in Action.20.10.17.
A48746. Pte Ingham   do.   19.10.17.
D40820. Pte Merrin.   do.   do.
D48392. "   Smith. F.   do.   do.

B33219. L/Cpl Ravenscroft. H. Wounded slightly at
                              Duty. 20.10.17.

SECRET.

WAR DIARY.
NOVEMBER 1917
16th Battalion Manchester Regiment.

VOLUME XXV.

..................Lieut-Colonel.
Commanding 16th Bn Manchester Regiment.

16 Manchesters Vol 25 (handwritten margin note)

SECRET.

Army Form C. 2118

WAR DIARY
or
INTELLIGENCE SUMMARY
16R (S) Bn Manchester Regt.
Volume XXV page 1
November

(Erase heading not required.)

Instructions regarding War Diaries and Intelligence Summaries are contained in F.S. Regs, Part II. and the Staff Manual respectively. Title Pages will be prepared in manuscript.

Place	Date	Hour	Summary of Events and Information	Remarks and references to Appendices
	1917 Nov 7-8		Relieved by 2nd Yorks in Left Sub sector (WYTSCHAETE) moved to Rearview Camps	
	11		Moved by march route to STRAZEELE	
	14		Entrained at STRAZEELE to STEENVOORDE (Training Area). Training to 24th R. Xmas weather having (intense)	
	24		Marched to ALBERTA CAMP. Brancardiere Co in Corps.	
	25		Relieved 11LF Cheshires front line (YPRES MENIN ROAD) Left sector Dispositions A Coy (Left Front) C Coy (Left Support) B Coy (Right Front) D Coy (Right Support) Relieved by 17th Manchesters in Front line. Moved into reserve trenches Top Team	
	29-30		CASUALTIES for month	
			Killed OFF.— OR—	Wounded 4
			MISSING 10 OR	22 (5 DIED OF WOUNDS) See Appendix I

W. Sisson Lt Colonel
Commanding 16R(S) Bn Manchester Regt.

WAR DIARY.
Appendix 1.

CASUALTIES. NOVEMBER 1917.

```
C7294.   Pte FAGAN J.         Killed in Action    8.11.17.
C51063   Pte REEVE E.         Killed in Action    25.11.17.

R43102.  P/Cpl BARSBY. J.        do.              28.11.17.

A302987  Pte SHERRY.J.           do.              28.11.17.
```

Died of Wounds.

```
C41862   Pte GODFREY.W.A.     Died of Wounds.    26.11.17.
C51056.  Pte PADGHAM.G.          Do.             28.11.17.
C49648   Pte CLARK.A.            do.             27.11.17.
```

Wounded in Action.

```
C6744    Pte GLEAVE W.B.      Wounded in Action.  8.11.17.
C7654    Pte PERELLI.J.          do               6.11.17 (At Duty.)
C43040   L/Cpl COX. J.           do.             25.11.17.
C23026   Pte Woolley.            do.              do.
C41862.   "   Godfrey W.A.       do.              do.
C41857.   "   Crimmins. W.       do.             26.11.17.
A245153. Pte Leak.R.             do.              do.
C51056.  Pte Padgham. G.         do.              do.
A49648.  Pte Clark.A.            do.              do.
A36952.  L/C. Roberts. G.H.      do.              do.
A6332.   Pte Woodburn. G.        do.              do.
A23096.  Pte Hart. W.            do.              do.
A51060.  Pte Richardson F.A.     do.              do.
D5099.   L/Sgt Bennett H.        do.              do.
D245132. Pte Heywood. W.S.       do.              do.
B245118. Pte Hindle. M.          do.             28.11.17.
D43026.  L/Cpl Irving. J.D.      do.              do.
B7219.   Pte Gibson H.           do.             29.11.17.
A19513.   "   Smith. J.          do.              do.
D35455.  Pte Crolla. F.          do.              do.
D43069.  Pte Haslingden. J.      do.              do.
A29426.  Pte Willcocks. B.R.     do.             28.11.17 at Duty.
```

MISSING.

```
B245147. Pte Kelly.          Missing In Action  5.11.17.
```

Webb. Lieut-Colonel.
Commanding 16th B Battⁿ Man Regt.

VOLUME XXVI

SECRET
....

WAR DIARY
FOR THE MONTH OF DECEMBER

16th BATTALION, MANCHESTER REGIMENT

January 3rd, 1918   ....Major
                       Commanding 16th Bn Manchester Regiment.

Army Form C. 2118.

WAR DIARY
INTELLIGENCE SUMMARY.
(Erase heading not required.)

16TH (S) BN. MANCHESTER RGT.

DECEMBER 1917

VOLUME XXVI — Page 1

Place	Date	Hour	Summary of Events and Information	Remarks and references to Appendices
	1917			
TORR TOP TUNNELS	Decr: 1-2		Batt. in Bde Reserve	
ALBERTA CAMP	3		Relieved by 20th K.L.R. & marched to ALBERTA CAMP.	
	4-11		Training & supplied working parties in forward area	
TRENCHES	12		Relieved 20th K.L.R. in Centre sub-sector. J.5 trenchline — GHELUVELT Trenches	
	13-14		Dispositions A. on left. C in centre D. on right — B in support	
			Batt. (less B. & D. Coys) relieved by 17th A/ck+b Rgt. & went into support at STIRLING CASTLE.	
STIRLING CASTLE	15			
SWAN CHATEAU	18		Relieved by 20th K.L.R. & marched to SWAN CHATEAU area.	
	19-26		Supplied working parties in front area.	
STIRLING CASTLE	24		Relieved 13th K.L.R. in Support position at STIRLING CASTLE.	
TRENCHES	27		Relieved 2nd R.S.F. in left sub-sector, POLDERHOEK Trenches.	
CHIPPEWA CAMP	30		Relieved by 20th K.L.R. & marched to CHIPPEWA WEST Camp.	
	31		Cleaning up.	
			AWARDS & HONOURS during the month	See Appendix I
			CASUALTIES during the month.	See Appendix II.
			Killed Wounded	
			O.R. 1 21	

Comdg 16th (S) Bn Mch Regt.

War Diary - December
Appendix I

16th Bn Manchester Regiment.

HONOURS & AWARDS.   December 1917

Lieut-Colonel W. ELSTOB M.C.	Mentioned in Despatches. Authority London Gazette d/18.12.17.
2/Lieut F. W. KEELING	" "
6333 Cpl WYNN W.	" "
A/6442 L/Sgt WALKER A.	Military Medal. Authority D.R.O. 3314 d/15.12.17.
A/6207 L/Sgt ARNFIELD T.	" "
C/41868 L/Cpl HODGSON P.	" "
A/40885 Pte WRIGHT G.	" "

WAR DIARY - DECEMBER 1917
Appendix II

CASUALTIES. BELGIUM. December 1917

A/24882 Pte DAVIDSON. Killed in Action 28.12.17.

D/51037 Pte HAYNES H.	Wounded Accidentally	1.12.17
B/250660 " CORLETT J.R.	" "	"
A/41820 L/Cpl WHYBERD E.W.	Wounded Slightly at Duty	2.12.17
D/33895 Pte MONTEVERDE.	Wounded in Action	14.12.17.
B/38699 Pte OGDEN A.	Wounded Accidentally	14.12.17
D/7055 Sgt SIMPSON G.	Wounded in Action	14.12.17.
D/41868 Pte HARVEY H.J.	" "	"
D/25876 " CHAPMAN J.	" "	"
D/252827 " GRIERSON W.H.	" "	"
A/245142 Pte JONES J.	" "	"
D/43063 Pte GOULBOURN W.	" "	25.12.17
B/20628 Pte GARDNER G.A.	" "	26.12.17
A/302774 " CUSACK H.	" "	28.12.17
C/51040 " HELMS H.	" "	"
B/3201 " HOBSON E.	" "	"
C/46817 " HOPKINSON A.H.	" "	"
B/6636 Cpl JOWLE R.	" "	"
B/37655 Pte STOCKTON L.	" "	"
A/31310 Pte WILD R.	" "	29.12.17
A/245139 Pte HODGSON R.	" "	"
C/51998 " ASHURST	" "	"

Capt E. N. ASHE buried in Dugout on 28th December
    admitted F.A. 30th December 1917 but not
    yet reported as Wounded.

Lieut R. E. OST buried in Dugout 28th December 1917
    and admitted F.A. suffering from shock but
    not yet reported Wounded.

VOLUME XXVII.

SECRET.

WAR DIARY
FOR THE MONTH OF JANUARY.
16TH. (S) BATTALION MANCHESTER REGIMENT.

February 1, 1918.   ......Gibbon...... MAJOR.
                        Commanding 16th. (S) Bn. Manchester Regiment.

WAR DIARY 1/6 (8)th MANCHESTER REGT.

JANUARY 1918

INTELLIGENCE SUMMARY

(Erase heading not required.)

Army Form C. 2118.

VOLUME XXVII. Page 1.

Place	Date 1918	Hour	Summary of Events and Information	Remarks and references to Appendices
CHIPPEWA CAMP	Jan. 1-4		Eliring up	
LYNDE	" 5		Conveyed by train from DICKEBUSCHE to EBBLINGHEM and marched to LYNDE.	
LA NEUVILLE	" 7		Entrained at STEENBECQUE, proceeded to LONGUEAU and marched to LA NEUVILLE	
	" 8-12		Training	
VAUVILLERS	" 13		Marched from LA NEUVILLE to VAUVILLERS.	
NESLE	" 14		Marched from VAUVILLERS to NESLE	
	" 15-18		Training	
ESMERY-HALLON	" 19		Marched from NESLE to ESMERY-HALLON. Training and reorganising	
SALENCY	" 26		Marched from ESMERY-HALLON to SALENCY	
SINCENY	" 28		Marched from SALENCY to SINCENY (BHQ, B&C Coys.) and PIERREMANDE (A&D Coys) being battalion in support on the extreme right of the British Army in France	See Appendix I
			AWARDS and HONOURS during the month	
			CASUALTIES during the month Killed Wounded	26.12.18
			Officers - 3	30.1.18
			O.R. - 1	

War Diary January 1918.
Appendix 1.

10th. BATTALION MANCHESTER REGIMENT.

HONOURS AND AWARDS.

Lieut-Colonel W. ELSTOB. M.C.	Awarded D.S.O. for distinguished service in the field. Authority London Gazette 1-1-18.
Major R. GIBBON.	Awarded Military Cross do.
Q.M. & Hon. Lieut J.T. BALL	Awarded Military Cross do.
Second Lieut W. McQUINN	Awarded Military Cross Authority IX Corps A/372340/5 dated 14-1-18.
7194. Sgt. Arrandale S.R.	Awarded Military Medal Auth. IX Corps A/372/45 dated 6-1-18.
3/01 Pte. HOBSON E.	do. do.
46817. Pte. HOPKINSON. A.H.	do. do.

In the field.
1-   -18.   ....MAJOR.
                        Cmdg. 10th. Battalion Manchester Regiment.

War Diary Jan. 1918.
Appendix 11.

16th. BATTALION MANCHESTER REGIMENT.

Casualties January 1918.

2/Lt. C.M. Hansard. Wounded in action 26-12-17
Capt. E.N. Ashe.   do.   26-12-17
Lieut. R.A Ost.   do.   26-12-17.

48346. Pte. J. Cook. attached Div. Salv. Coy
                Wounded.   30-1-18.

In the field.
31-1-18.

                      .... MAJOR.
                      Cmdg. 16th. Bn. Manchester Regiment.

VOLUME XXVIII

S E C R E T

W A R   D I A R Y
FOR THE MONTH OF FEBRUARY
16th (S) BN MANCHESTER REGIMENT

28th February 1918 ....Major
Commanding 16th Bn Manchester Regiment.

Army Form C. 2118.

WAR DIARY
or
INTELLIGENCE SUMMARY.
(Erase heading not required.)

16th Bn Manchester Regt

February 1918

Instructions regarding War Diaries and Intelligence Summaries are contained in F.S. Regs., Part II. and the Staff Manual respectively. Title pages will be prepared in manuscript.

Place	Date	Hour	Summary of Events and Information	Remarks and references to Appendices
LES BUTTES DE ROUPY	1.2.18		B.H.Q. B and C Coys marched from SINCENY to LES BUTTES DE ROUPY (A+D Coys remaining at PIERREMAND) until the 2nd week when they marched to SINCENY) From 28.1.18 to 8.2.18 the Bn was in Brigade Reserve and provided working parties (chiefly for wiring) under direction of R.E.s	Honours and Awards See APPENDIX I
	6.2.18		Draft of 13 officers and 280 o.r. joined the Bn from 19th Bn Manchester Regt on account of the redistribution of units at this time. The 18th were taken out of the Brigade and eventually became the 17th Entrenching Bn. At the same time the 17th Bn Manchester Regt was transferred from 90th to 21st Bde	
	7.2.18		The Commanding Officer welcomed the draft from the 19th Bn Manchester Regt in the Y.M.C.A. hut at SINCENY. (See Appendix II)	APPENDIX II
MANICAMP	8.2.18		The Bn was relieved by the 2/1st Bn London Regt (58th Division) and marched to MANICAMP	
QUESMY	10.2.18		marched from MANICAMP to QUESMY	
OGNOLLES	11.2.18		marched from QUESMY to OGNOLLES	
	13.2.18		Division inspected by Commander-in-Chief (F.M. Sir Douglas Haig) at EREHEU. (General Salute and March Past in Column of Platoons)	
	15.2.18		A and D Coys and No 8 Platoon (B.Coy) marched from OGNOLLES to CURCHY for work on railway and remained on this fatigue until 1.3.18	
HAM	20.2.18		The Bn (less A+D Coys and No 8 Platoon) marched from OGNOLLES to HAM	
ETREILLERS	22.2.18		The Bn (less A+D Coys and No 8 Platoon) marched from HAM to ETREILLERS	
	28.2.18		A and D Coys and No 8 Platoon joined the Bn 1.3.18. At this period the Bn was in Brigade Reserve, working on Defensive positions, digging trenches &c	
			HONOURS and AWARDS during the month, NIL. CASUALTIES NIL	APPENDIX I

R.W.Ulan Major
Comand 16 Bn Manchester Regt

War Diary February 1918
APPENDIX I

16th (3) Bn Manchester Regiment.

HONOURS AND AWARDS

A/43046 R.S.M. POTTER W.J.   Awarded BELGIAN CROIX DE GUERRE
                               for Gallantry.

D/7055 Sgt SIMPSON G.   -ditto-

                               Authority. M.S./11/7519 d/27.1.18.
                                          IXth Corps Letter
                                          A/372/394 d/27.1.18

In the field.   ....Major
28. 2. 18   Commanding 16th Bn Manchester Regiment.

16th Bn Manchester Regiment

The Commanding Officer's Address to Officers, N.C.Os and men of the 19th Bn Manchester Regiment on 7.2.18.

Captains ASHE, HUNTER, HEYWOOD, GUEST, SHARPLES and padre also present.

I arranged for you all to come here this morning as it is rather a special occasion.

You officers, N.C.Os and men of the 19th Bn Manchester Regiment must feel pretty sick at your Battalion being split up and believe me that very natural feeling is appreciated by us all. Higher authorities, however, have decided on a re-organisation of the formation of the Army and, as all alterations and innovations do, it is bound to hit somebody or other pretty hard for a time though it is all done with great hopes of improvement in fighting efficiency.

Fighting is what we are all here for and the only way of fighting well is to have good organization. It is, therefore, up to us all to enter heart and soul into the new organization, make it a big success and by so doing lick the Boche.

Your Battalion is part and parcel of us - you were formed at the same time that we were - you trained in England in the same areas that we did. When the 90th Bde was formed it consisted of the 16th, 17th, 18th and 19th Battalions of the Manchester Regt and we came out to France in November 1915 in that formation.

Shortly after arrival the 19th Battalion was transferred to the 21st Bde in accordance with principles laid down by G.H.Q. At that time we were quite disappointed, to say the least of it. It was quite like parting from an old friend and, I'll whisper it quietly, efforts have been made on several occasions to get you back to this Bde.

Though in different Brigades we have fought together on the SOMME, near ARRAS and at YPRES - where the 19th have been, so have the 16th and vice-versa.

Your Commanding Officer - Col MACDONALD, as you know was originally Adjutant of the 17th Battalion and is known and admired by us all. It is a real pleasure to greet troops who have been under his command.

I dont want to bore you with a long speech but from the foregoing I hope I have made it clear that we do not regard you as strangers come amongst us - very much to the contrary - you are old friends who have rejoined us again.

The number of your Battalion may have been different to ours but after all the second figure of either one or the other only needs to do a somersault and it becomes the same. Above all we are the same Regiment. A Regiment with fine traditions and fine Battle honours to which both the 16th and 19th Battalions have added in no small measure since arriving in France.

I will conclude therefore by giving you on behalf of COL. ELSTOB, who is at present on Leave, and all ranks a most hearty welcome to our Battalion with a sincere hope that you will not find it difficult to settle down and regard the 16th your own Battalion.

90th Inf.Bde.
30th Div.

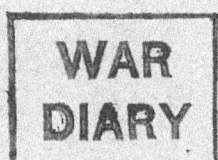

16th BATTN. THE MANCHESTER REGIMENT.

M A R C H

1 9 1 8

Attached:-

Appendices I, II & III.

VOLUME XXIX

WAR DIARY
For the Month of March 1918.
16th (S) Battalion Manchester Regiment.

31.3.18.
................................2/Lieut.
Commanding 16th Bn Manchester Regt.

Army Form O. 1810
All Arms.

Each issue of Orders will be numbered consecutively throughout the year. A fresh series will be commenced with the first issue in each year.

Unit _____

DAILY ORDERS. PART II.

N.B.—The Sub. No. of Order and Subject are to be shown in Columns 1 and 2 thus:—1—Courts-Martial.

Station _____

No. _____
Date _____

Regimental No., Rank, and Name.	Sqdn., Batty., or Co.	Particulars of Casualties, etc., and Date.

Officer Commanding or Adjutant.

Army Form C. 2118.

WAR DIARY
or
INTELLIGENCE SUMMARY 16/D Manchester Regiment.
(Erase heading not required.)

March 1918.

Place	Date	Hour	Summary of Events and Information	Remarks and references to Appendices
In the field	1/3/18		The Battalion was in Reserve at ETREILLERS and engaged in the work of constructing defences. Working parties organized and standing	Casualties — See Appx I
ETREILLERS	3/3/18		to Battle positions practised.	
Front of ST QUENTIN	5/3/18 to 17/3/18		Relieved 17 2nd B" Yorkshire Regt. and proceeded to BELLS at AUBERT in Bgde Reserve. "C" Coy proceeded to DOUCHY on Working Party on 7th inst. Remainder of Battalion also engaged on road working parties.	Unknown See Appx II
	17/3/18		Battalion less D Coy moved to SAVY DUG OUTS. D Coy ETREILLER Defences.	
	19/3/18		Bn moved to front line relieving 17th MCRS. A Coy 16th relieved B Coy 17th MCRS. Rt front Coy. D Coy 16 MCRS relieved A Coy 17th MCRS Left front Coy. C Coy 16 MCRS relieved C Coy 17th MCRS in Counter attack Coy. D Coy 16 MCRS relieved D Coy 17th MCRS - Savane Defence Coy, HQ in Manchester Redoubt.	
	21/3/18	4.30 a.m.	German Grand attack on	See Appx III
	31/3/18		Remaining front of Bn concentrated at BOUBERT for re-organization. Working towards 2/construction to concentrating 16th Bn Manchester	

A P P E N D I C E S

I, II and III .

16th Bn Manchester Regiment.   War Diary, Mch. 1918.
                                Appendix 1.

Casualty Report in accordance with 90th Bde C22.

Officers.

Killed.	Wounded.	Missing.
	Major R.E.Roberts.	Lieut-Col W. Elstob D.S.O. M.C.
	Lt & Q.M.J.T.Rall.	
	2/Lt J.W.Barton.	Major R. Gibbon, M.C.
	2/Lt G.A.Taylor.	Capt N Sharples.
	2/Lt H.Kelly.	Capt E.N.Ashe.
		A/Capt J. Guest.
		Capt O.T.Prichard.
		A/Capt P.H.Heywood.
		Lieut J.Clarke.
		2/Lt J.A.Bentley.
		2/Lieut M.D.Pleasance.
		2/Lieut W.Dean.
		2/Lieut W. McQuinn.
		2/Lieut C.Lewis.
		2/Lieut F.W.Keeling.
		2/Lieut F.Hayes.
		2/Lieut J.A.Birchenough.
		2/Lieut F.J.Durrant.
		2/Lieut W.F.J.Hall M.C.

2/Lieut A.C.Abba and 2/Lieut J.A.Ellis were
admitted F.A. on 21.3.18 suffering from effects
of the Battle but it is not known if they
have been diagnosed as Battle Casualties.

Major R.E.Roberts is unofficially reported
as having Died of Wounds.

Lieut-Colonel W.Elstob is unofficially reported

wounded and Missing.

16th Bn Manchester Regiment.   Sheet 2.

Casualty List. Other Ranks.

Killed.   Wounded.   Missing.

 ----   8.   593.

The above are the casualties for the action 21.3.18
to 25.3.18.   These figures are as correct as can
be ascertained at present.

                            W.H.Smithbank 2/Lieut.
1.4.18.   Commanding 16th Bn Manchester Regt.

War Diary March 1918
Appendix 11.

16th Bn Manchester Regiment.

Honours and Awards.

N I L.

In the Field.
1.4.18.

........Brittlebank........ 2/Lieut
Commanding 16th Bn Manchester Regt

War Diary March 1918
Appendix lll

TO,
   G.O.C. 90 Brigade.

From,
   O.C. 16th(S) Bn Manchester Regiment.

SIR, I have the honour to submit to you an account of the fighting by this battalion from 4,30 a.m March 21st 1918 to March 28th 1918 inclusive.

Our patrol left No 2 Outpost at 2 a.m and reported no enemy activity was observed. Enemy Barrage opened at 4,30 a.m. approx. Gas was freely used. Shelling was chiefly between outpost line and line of resistance received most enemy attention. At the same time a Box Barrage was placed on the back Area of ETREILLERS.

The Bombardment continued till 11 a.m. when our Artillery shortened range and pounded our own line of resistance, which was still occupied by our Troops in places.

Boche Troops were then observed on our Left Flank advancing from ridge beyond the Old Roman Road and later on were seen advancing in Mass along the Sunken Road to the right of MANCHESTER REDOUBT. Our first Troops to be engaged were those in MANCHESTER REDOUBT at 10.30 a.m.

Under cover of the Mist the Bosche was able to advance within Bombing distance of the REDOUBT. Daylight S.O.S was sent up but not observed. Some of our posts then retired on the REDOUBT. The Bosche was held for a time by Rifle Fire ; the Vickers Gun in the Redoubt being at this stage out of Action. By this time the REDOUBT was completely surrounded but continued to put up a stout resistance. Alternative Battle Positions were then manned. All papers of value to the Enemy had been destroyed. The REDOUBT fell in the course of the afternoon. The front Line was attacked from the Rear.

To my knowledge no Frontal Attack was launched.

Stragglers were collected by 2/Lieut F.J.SMITH N of ETREILLERS and at 8 p.m reported to Brigade at VAUX and proceeded to VILLERS ST CHRISTOPHE.

On the 23rd the BN manned positions on the _ Canal . No Enemy Action was observed til Mid-Day 24th March when Enemy movement was observed on the Sky line immediately to our front Troops were seen moving across under cover of

Sheet 2.
the wood in frot of GRECOURT to the village of HOMBLEUX.
It was thought Enemy Troops were massing here to storm the bridge at O.5 d 25.65. (Ref sheet 66 d)
This continued at intervals and many casualties were inflicted by rifle fire. At 5 p.m. the Enemy shelled our positions heavily but with little result; There was no known Enemy Action during the night.
On the 25th March our Troops brought heavy Rifle Fire to bear on Enemy Troops moving across our Front. At 5,30 it was noticed that both our Flanks had given way. An attempt was made under MAJOR R.E ROBERTS to hold up the right Flank till it was seen that ther was a danger of being surrounded, when all Troops retired on the village of CRESSY. Outpost positions were taken up here, and patrols were sent forward. No Enemy Troops were encountered. In the course of the night our Troops retired through ROYE on the village of BOUCHOIR when positions were manned by the BN at the QUARRIES at K 22 a.2.8. (Ref Sheet 66 E) on the 26th March.
There was no Action till 11 a.m 27th Mch, when the Bn was ordered to re- inforce the right Flank.
At this stage the QUARRIES were heavily shelled, a number of casualties being sustained. Two waves were formed and advanced through the troops retiring from our front and Support Line and positions were taken up in the line of Trenches W of the Village of BOUCHOIR. The Order was then received to hold Line at K.22.b.2.5. (Ref 66 E) positions covering our left Flank had been taken up at this stage. In the course of the afternoon efforts were made to advance out of the Village of BOUCHOIR. Owing to heavy Machine Gun fire these were unavailing.
There was no further Action during the night.
On the 28th Mch at 9,30 am the Village of ARVILLERS was evacuated, and our Troops held their positions till 11,30 a.m. The Left Flank then retired and the BN retired by order of Brigade through French Troops.
The Bn formed up and marched back to ROUVREL.

I have the honour to be.
    SIR.
        Your obedient servant.
            W. Rosslebank 2/Lieutenant
            Commanding 16th BN Manchester Regiment

2.4.18

Confidential.

90/30

War Diary
of
1.6" Bn. Manchester Regt.
for month of
APRIL 1915.

VOLUME XXX.

SECRET

WAR   DIARY
for the month of April 1918.
16th (S) Battalion Manchester Regiment.

30.4.18.

W H Colley   Major, Commanding,
16th Battalion Manchester Regiment.

Army Form C. 2118.

WAR DIARY
or
INTELLIGENCE SUMMARY.
(Erase heading not required.)

Instructions regarding War Diaries and Intelligence Summaries are contained in F. S. Regs., Part II. and the Staff Manual respectively. Title pages will be prepared in manuscript.

Place	Date	Hour	Summary of Events and Information	Remarks and references to Appendices
FEUQUIERES	5/14/18	3 p.m.	Battn. entrained at 3.0 p.m. and detrained at ROUSBRUGGE at 6 p.m. and proceeded by bus to camp at	
		noon	INTERNATIONAL CORNER	
KEMPTON PARK	7/14/18		Battn. marched to KEMPTON PARK and came under orders of Reserve. Major W.H. COTTER, 2nd Battn.	
			Yorkshire Regt. assumed command of the Battn.	
GOURNIER FARM	12/14/18	3 p.m.	Battn. moved Battle positions. Battn. H.Q. being at GOURNIER FARM	
	16/14/18	6 a.m.	All troops formed up. Battn. was within one mile of the STEENBEEKE clearing the Battn. as the	
			front line. One Company of the 17th Bn. Manchester Regt. reinforced the line	
MOULON CAMP	17/14/18		The Battn. was relieved by 2 Coys of 13th Belgian Infantry Regt. One and ½ Battn. marched to	
			MOULON CAMP near ELVERDINGHE	
ST.LAWRENCE CAMP	18/14/18		The Battn. marched to ST LAWRENCE CAMP	
SPOIL BANK	19/14/18		The Battn. was formed into two Coys and with the 17th Bn. Manchester Regt. also H.Q. (to be formed into two Coys) formed a Composite Battn. under the command of the 16th Bn. H.Q. The	
			Battn. marched to camp at BUSSEBOOM and from there to the front line at SPOIL BANK	
			(on South side of YPRES-COMINES CANAL) relieving two Coys of 6th Battn. Cameronns	
	20/14/18		The Battn. was relieved in the front line by No 3 Battn. 39th Composite Brigade. On relief the	
			Battn. moved to close support at SPOIL BANK and LOCK 8.	

Army Form C. 2118.

WAR DIARY
or
INTELLIGENCE SUMMARY.
(Erase heading not required.)

Instructions regarding War Diaries and Intelligence Summaries are contained in F. S. Regs., Part II, and the Staff Manual respectively. Title pages will be prepared in manuscript.

Place	Date	Hour	Summary of Events and Information	Remarks and references to Appendices
SPOIL BANK	25.4.18	10 a.m.	The enemy attacked South of YPRES-COMINES CANAL and one Coy of the Batln counter	
			attacked to restore the situation and two Coys formed a defensive flank from SHELLEY FARM	See
			- VOORMEZEELE	APPENDIX I
"	26.4.18	9.30 a.m.	In a thick mist the enemy overran the forward posts and drove the remnants of the	
			Batln from SPOIL BANK to LOCK 8 where a line was held, the Batln being absorbed in 39th	
			Batln 39th Composite Brigade	
SCOTTISH CAMP	27.4.18 28.4.18 29.4.18		Various parties came back from the line and reformed at SCOTTISH CAMP. No formal	
			relief took place	
	29.4.18		The Batln (less HQ) was formed into a composite Company and attached to 2nd Bn Yorkshire	
			Regt. The composite Coy proceeded to man trenches near OUDERDOM. HQ and details joined	
			Transport lines near POPERINGHE (L 10 central Sheet 27)	
			From 19th inst. to the end of the month the 17th Batln Manchester Regt (less HQ) remained	
			with the Batln forming a composite Batln.	

W. H. Cotty(?)
Major
Commanding 17th Bn Manchester Regt

L.B.A.   C3.

Ref. your B.M.110 d/28.4.18.

On the night of 24/25 April 1918, VWD was relieved by P.C.(No.2 Composite Bn of the 39th Div). On relief the Bn was disposed as under:-

    D Coy.   Tunnel near Norfolk Bridge.
    A "   )
    Bn H.Q.)   Spoil Bank.
    B Coy.   Lock 7.
    C "   "   8.

About 10 a.m. on the morning of 25th April P.C. was heavily attacked by the enemy, who forced their line back to the line BLUFF-OOSTHOEK FARM - SHELLEY FARM - MOUND.
I received verbal orders from P.A. to counter attack on the left of the line south of the CANAL with one of my Coys and to form a defensive flank with 2 Coys on the line MOUND - WHITEHORSE CELLARS - VOORMEZEELE. Telephonic communication with LBA was broken and knowing my Bn was in reserve for the North of the Canal I was at a loss what to do.   I rang up PA and was informed that LBA had given their permission and were sending written instructions. These did not arrive until after I had taken action in accordance with PA instructions.   D Coy made a counter attack and re-established the situation in the neighbourhood of OOSTHOEK. B & C Coys were detailed for the defensive flank and the Coy commanders at once went out to reconnoitre, getting into touch with C.O. of SEAFORTHS and No.4 Composite Bn of the 39th Division on the right.   C Coy was distributed in depth with its left on ST.101 - THREE KINGS ROAD.   B Coy in depth with its right on this road and its left on SHELLEY FARM, the MOUND being by this time in the hands of the enemy.   I handed over D Coy and one platoon of B Coy to the C.O. of P.C. for tactical purposes and that night he visited his line from the BLUFF to SHELLEY FARM and I the posts of B & C Coys.   Coys were in touch along the whole front, but the new positions were somewhat isolated and had no wire in front of them. I kept LBB and VWB continually informed of the situation. About 9.30 a.m. on the 26th April the enemy put down a heavy barrage on and behind our posts and as the morning was misty in addition to the usual Bn O.P. of 1 N.C.O. and 3 men, I put an officer's guard on the south entrance to the SPOIL BANK Tunnel.
A Coy had standing orders that in case the enemy broke through they were without further orders to issue forth from the south side of the Tunnel and take up a line approx. ARUNDLE FARM - NORFOLK LODGE. They had practised clearing the tunnel and had all got clear in two minutes.   This morning the men were standing to continuously. About 10 a.m. news was brought to me and C.O. of P.C. who happened to be with me in SPOIL BANK that the enemy were approaching SPOIL BANK. I immediately went out on the north side of the Tunnel and warned A Coy to turn out and my Second-in-Command to get Bn H.C. out. I then went to the top of the bank and saw the enemy about 60 yds away approaching from the direction of NORFOLK LODGE - OOSTHOEK. The C.O. of PC came to the top of the bank with me and then left me saying he was going to try and organise a counter attack from the direction of the SPOIL BANK Dressing Station along the south side of the Canal. No news was received from our front that the enemy were breaking through and A Coy Commander had no time to turn out more than two platoons on the south side of the SPOIL BANK, most of whom were either killed or wounded.   The probable reasons why A Coy did not get out more quickly were :-
(1). The heavy barrage round the tunnel entrance did not lift until the enemy had M.Gs playing on the entrances. I manned the top of the bank until an enemy M.G. from near NORFOLK BRIDGE enfiladed the position, causing heavy casualties.   I then took about 50 men across the Canal to the North bank which I lined, suffering heavily in doing so. Other parties of men went down towards Lock 8. M.G. fire rendered my position on the Northern bank untenable and I withdrew to rising ground North of the Canal with greatly reduced numbers. Here my party suffered in a barrage and was reduced to about 10. I found some trenches occupied by a Coy of VWB and after a consultation with the Coy commander we decided he should counter attack at once. He was advancing to the attack when he received a message from Lt.Col. Wynne to line the Canal Bank from Lock 7 to Lock 8, which he did. I then sent an officer to LBB to explain the situation and I went to BEDFORD HOUSE to report to LBA. Here I discovered that my

sheet 2.

second-in-command had about 20 men with him at LOCK 8 and I was ordered to report to Major NADEN, O.C. 4th Composite Bn at VOORMEZEELE and help him to man the line LOCK 8 - VOORMEZEELE. I found his H.Q. in an open trench in No.1 G.H.Q. line and he informed me that about 100 of my men had been driven back into his front line. I visited them that night and found they numbered 60-70 men and 5 officers, chiefly of B & C Coys. I spent the night 26/27 in No.1 G.H.Q. line which was badly shelled during the next day. On the night 27/28 acting on Major NADENS instructions I went back to SCOTTI H CAMP as he had arranged all details for the relief of the Bn, the whole line being under his orders.
At the present moment remnants of B & C Coys who have not yet been relieved are, I am informed, still in the front line and have beaten back enemy attacks, also bombing raids from the direction of LOCK 8. It would seem that the enemy broke through near TRIANGULAR WOOD and rolled up my left flank, but it is difficult to obtain definite news as no Coy officers are yet back from the line. No news of D Coy has been received since the action.

29.4.18.

(Sgd) W.H.COLLEY, Major,
Commanding VWD.

TO
LBA.
E313.

In continuation of my narrative of the action of my Battalion during the recent fighting, I have now had an opportunity of ascertaining from my Coy officers further details of what occurred. On the 27th April, apart from two heavy barrages during the day, which inflicted casualties, no attack was made.

The line ran from Lock 8 to CONVENT LANE and was held by 80 of our men and 50 of No.4 Composite Bn. About 9 p.m. the enemy were heard talking on the North Bank of the Canal - a patrol of the Black Watch under 2/Lt O.H. Dinnis was sent to get in touch with the Leicesters on the left. The patrol reported that no one was holding the posts on our left flank. It was subsequently ascertained that the enemy, in strong force, had broken through on our left. Our force being insufficient to attempt a counter attack, a defensive flank was formed along the South Bank of the Canal. A Coy of the Leicesters reinforced this flank but were subsequently withdrawn, once more leaving the left flank in the air except for a few isolated posts. This part of the line should have been relieved that evening, but no relief arrived. The next day all was quiet until about noon, when the enemy was observed advancing in single file in large numbers towards the right flank. Our fire enfiladed them, inflicting heavy casualties. The attack broke through our line on our right front, leaving our right flank in the air. About 5 p.m. a heavy barrage was put down destroying the trenches and driving our men towards Lock 8. About 7 p.m. we were compelled to withdraw about 200 yds to trenches occupied by the Leicesters, both flanks being still in the air.

The remnants of the Bn came out of the line, 3 officers and 12 O.Rs.

1.5.18.

(Sgd) W.H.Colley, Major,
Commanding 16th Manchester Regt.

Appendix 11.

War Diary — 16th Bn Manchester Regiment.

HONOURS & AWARDS

Italian Silver Medal for Military Valour — 2/Lt F.W. KEELING.

Distinguished Conduct Medal — 12453 L/Cpl SALTER F.

Military Cross. —
2/Lt W.G. BRITTLEBANK.
2/Lt T. HAWKINS.
2/Lt F.J. SMITH.

Military Medal. —
48527 Pte TOPPING J.
23109 " MANGER J.
40899 " BARTLES J.
35488 " DEAN J.
48668 " LUTMAN H.J.
11910 L/Sgt PILKINGTON A.E.
41846 Pte BATCHELOR A.
7091 Sgt COLEMAN A. (Bar to M.M.)
48495 A/C.S.M. SHEARD T.S.

War Diary. 16th Bn Manchester Regt. Appendix 111.

CASUALTIES.

2/Lt. W.E.J.Hall,	Wounded in Action. 25/27.4.18.
2/Lt. E.H.Noakes.	-do- -do-
2/Lt A.D.Turner.	-do- -do-
2/Lt G.H.Dinnis.	-do- & Missing. -do-
2/Lt F.S.Shaw.	Missing in Action 26.4.18.
2/Lt. E.Jones.	-do-
2/Lt H.T.Ringham.	-do-
2/Lt A.Woodacre.	-do-
2/Lt E.Bradwell.	-do-

Other Ranks.

Killed.	Wounded.	Missing.
3.	38.	195.

Index..........................

SUBJECT.

16th Manchester Regt.

No.	Contents.	Date.
	May 1918	

SECRET.   VOLUME XXXI.

WAR DIARY.

For the month of May, 1918.

16th (S) Battalion MANCHESTER REGIMENT.

31.5.18.   W.H.Bodley....Lieut-Colonel
                                                  Commanding
                                                  16th. Manchester Regt.

Army Form C.2118.

16th (S) Bn Manchester Regiment
WAR DIARY
or
INTELLIGENCE SUMMARY.
(Erase heading not required.)

Instructions regarding War Diaries and Intelligence
Summaries are contained in F. S. Regs., Part II.
and the Staff Manual respectively. Title pages
will be prepared in manuscript.

Place	Date	Hour	Summary of Events and Information	Remarks and references to Appendices
STEENVOORDE	2.5.18		Battn. less Company attached 2nd Bn Yorkshire Regt., moved by road to bivouacs outside STEENVOORDE.	
BUYSCHEERE	3.5.18		Do Do do BUYSCHEERE.	
"	10.5.18		The Company attached 2nd Bn Yorkshire Regt rejoined the Battn.	
"	13.5.18		The Battn was reduced to a training cadre of 10 officers and 49 O.R. with a view to the cadre being attached to an American Battn to assist in their training. Surplus transport and transport personnel was despatched to camp at CUCQ SOMPIN near ETAPLES for disposal	
"	14.5.18		Personnel surplus to training cadre was despatched to H.3.B.D. ETAPLES for disposal. The Band remained with the cadre for the time being.	
MONTHIERES	15/16.5.18		Training cadre and band moved by road to AUDRUICQ entraining there at 7.39 p.m. arriving at WOINCOURT at 7.30 a.m. 16th May. Training Cadre and Band then moved by road to MONTHIERES and became affiliated to the 1st Battn 140th Regiment United States Army	APPENDIX I
MONCHAUX	17.5.18		Training Cadre and band moved by road to MONCHAUX	
"	.5.18		The Battn Band was selected to become the Divisional Band but remained with the Battn until the end of the month.	APPENDIX II

Honours and Awards

Casualties during month :-

Killed	Died of Wounds	Wounded
1 Officer		2 Officers
3 O.R.	1 O.R.	20 O.R.

W. H. Colley
Lieut Colonel
Commanding
16th (S) Bn Manchester Regt.

WAR DIARY.   16th Manchester Regiment.   APPENDIX I

HONOURS & AWARDS.

MENTIONED IN DESPATCHES.

Captain R.K. KNOWLES.

DISTINGUISHED CONDUCT MEDAL.

26519 C.S.M. GILBERT. J

MILITARY MEDAL.

2850 Sgt THOMPSON .G.H.

39448 Sgt GRIMSHAW. H.

277745 L/Cpl WATERHOUSE. W.M.

26580 Pte COLLINS. G

W A R   D I A R Y.   16th. Manchester Regiment.   APPENDIX II.

CASUALTIES.

KILLED IN ACTION.   2/Lieut S. FINDLAY.   8.5.18.
                           57360 pte TASSELL W   3.5.18
                           57341 pte LANDERYOU J   -"-
                           47897 pte HATTON J   9.5.18.

DIED OF WOUNDS..   60670 C.S.M. COLLINS W'd 8.5.18
                                 F.G.

WOUNDED IN ACTION.   Captain G.M.HUNTER.   8.5.18.
                           2/Lieut W.G.BRITTLEBANK
                                (Now A/Capt)
                                Remained at Duty   8.5.18
                           40939 pte WREN G   )
                           29484 pte WILKINS W   )
                           11083 L/Cpl WHITELEY   )
                           48768   "   NUTTALL J)
                           40837 pte NASH WE   )
                           302065 L/Cpl MOORES H)
                           245154 " LEVISTON P) 3/9.5.18.
                           32362 pte BATTMAN A   )
                           37121 " MORRIS W   )
                            1549 " LOMAS   F   )
                           41842 " PUDDEY C   )
                           203125 " RIGBY G   )
                           57360 " BROOKE A   )
                           42597 L/Cpl BIRD A   )
                           52028 pte MELLOR J   )
                           51049 L/Cpl LIGO F   )
                            2016 Cpl METCALF A   )
                           43781 Sgt BARON E   )
                           39889 L/Cpl POWNER W   )
                           245820 "   LUND N.R.)

90th Brigade
30th Division.

Battalion was transferred to 14th Division 16.6.18

CONFIDENTIAL

WAR DIARY

OF

16th Manchester Regt.

FROM 1-6-18 TO 30-6-18.

VOLUME NO. 32.

Army Form C. 2118.

16th (S) Bn Manchester Regt. WAR DIARY for month of June 1918.

or

INTELLIGENCE SUMMARY.

(Erase heading not required.)

Instructions regarding War Diaries and Intelligence Summaries are contained in F. S. Regs., Part II. and the Staff Manual respectively. Title pages will be prepared in manuscript.

Place	Date	Hour	Summary of Events and Information	Remarks and references to Appendices
MONCHAUX	1.6.18		The 1st Batt. 440th Regt U.S. Army ceased to be attached to the Training Cadre.	
Do	1.6.18		The 3rd Batt 119th Regt U.S. Army arrived at MONCHAUX and became attached to the training	
			cadre for training.	
PAZINVAL	4.6.18		The Training Cadre with the affiliated U.S. Batts moved by road to PAZINVAL	
GAMACHES	16.6.18 9pm		A training cadre entrained for at GAMACHES for BOULOGNE. The Band was despatched	
			to H Depot, ETAPLES.	
BOULOGNE	16.6.18 5.4pm		A Training cadre arrived in BOULOGNE and spent the night at OSTROHOVE Rest Camp.	
			The Batt was transferred to the 14th Division (third Infantry Brigade)	
			The Batt entrained at BOULOGNE and disentrained at FOLKESTONE proceeding by train	
COWSHOT CAMP	17.6.18		to BROOKWOOD Station and from there to Camp at COWSHOT CAMP	
BROOKWOOD				
			The Batt. received various drafts of Bt and B.ii Officers and men during the remainder of the month.	
			Honours and Awards during month :- Capt E. N ASHE. Military Cross.	
			40993 Pte G. DEDEMEADE Distinguished Conduct Medal.	
			Casualties during month :- Nil	

W. A. Ridley .... LIEUT. COLONEL
Commanding 16th Service Bn. Manchester Regiment.

WAR DIARY. 16TH BN MANCHESTER REGIMENT. APPENDIX 1.

HONOURS & AWARDS.

MILITARY CROSS.

Captain E. N. ASHE.

DISTINGUISHED CONDUCT MEDAL.

40903 Private DODDEMEADE G.

....

www.ingramcontent.com/pod-product-compliance
Lightning Source LLC
Chambersburg PA
CBHW081355160426
43192CB00013B/2410